Andy Pruitt's Medical Guide for Cyclists

By Andrew L. Pruitt, Ed.D., with Fred Matheny
Photography by Nico Toutenhoofd
Cover design by Mike Shaw

RBR Publishing Company

PLEASE READ THIS!

Bicycling is a potentially dangerous activity. Crashes and accidents with motor vehicles are possible. Death can result.

Bikes can exceed 50 mph on descents. But even slow-speed crashes can lead to serious injury.

Some of you may decide to race or ride in large groups on tours or charity rides. Riding in a pack presents additional dangers. Because some riders aren't as skilled or as careful as others, they can involve you in a crash.

Please be careful while riding. Always wear a helmet, gloves and eye protection. Obey traffic laws. Don't get caught up in the excitement of the moment and ride dangerously, whether in a race, event or training ride.

The information in this book will help you avoid overuse injuries, but it can't protect you from crashes caused by inattention, equipment failure, or other dangers you will meet on bike paths, streets and highways.

We hope you want to enjoy the wonderful sport of cycling for many years. Do it safely with a full understanding and acceptance of its dangers.

©2001 by Andrew L. Pruitt. All rights reserved.

Published by RBR Publishing Company, 3141 Forest Knolls Dr., Chapel Hill, NC 27516, USA. www.RoadBikeRider.com.

Second printing, January 2002.

ISBN 0-9714619-0-2

RBR Publishing Company
EXPERT "HOW TO" INFORMATION FOR AVID CYCLISTS

Table of Contents

Forward

By Chris Carmichael, President
Carmichael Training Systems

I first met Andy Pruitt in 1981 when I was a young racer suffering from a stabbing pain along the side of my knee. Andy was the Head Athletic Trainer at the University of Colorado, and for Boulder's expanding population of elite athletes, he was rapidly gaining a reputation as the medical professional to see if you had overuse injuries that no one else could fix.

Andy told me I had "ilio-tibial band friction syndrome." It was the first time I'd ever heard this term. With his treatment, the symptoms vanished quickly.

But unlike other medical pros I had seen, he was more interested in what was *causing* my symptoms. He carefully checked my position on the bike and modified it. I never had that injury again.

All through his career, Andy's focus has been on finding and preventing the causes of injury.

When I started coaching, I sent my U.S. National Cycling Team athletes to Andy. Over the years, he worked with Lance Armstrong, Chann McRae, Fred Rodriguez—all the riders who are at the top of the sport today.

His medical expertise is now legendary. He pioneered video analysis to determine bike fit. He has worked with Lance to increase his flexibility so he can achieve a more aerodynamic time trial position. The 1994 Worlds were in Sicily, where it was extremely hot. Karen Kurreck was suffering from dehydration, but Andy solved the problem and Karen won the World Time Trial Championship.

Andy was never too busy to help. He never turned away an athlete because his appointment roster was filled or failed to return my phone calls because he was too involved with his own practice.

Andy can take his own advice, too. When we went to Colombia for the World Championships, he set up a detailed program so the riders wouldn't get sick. It worked. The cyclists stayed healthy. Andy didn't get sick, either—but he spent most of his time treating the staff. We had been so busy telling riders not to drink the water that we had forgotten to take care of ourselves!

Above all, Andy always puts the athlete first.

He was the Chief Medical Officer for U.S. Cycling when we were preparing for the 1996 Olympics. We wanted to use narrow bottom brackets on our time trial bikes for better aerodynamics, so Andy devised force-measuring pedals to see if riders could produce as much power with their feet closer together than in their normal stance.

But Andy wasn't just interested in power production. He also wanted to see if a narrow stance would cause injuries that might lead to long-term problems. He was looking beyond the riders' performances in Atlanta and focusing on their health for the rest of their lives. That approach is the measure of the man.

I'm happy that Andy has finally compiled his knowledge about cycling injuries in a book. He is unique among the world's cycling medicine experts because he can diagnose and treat cycling problems for everyone—recreational as well as elite cyclists.

If you love to ride and want to continue for your whole life, the information in this book is priceless.

Introduction

By Fred Matheny, Coauthor
www.RoadBikeRider.com

As Chris Carmichael notes, the advice and wisdom in this book comes from Andy Pruitt's medical training and years of experience working with elite and recreational cyclists.

To convert Andy's knowledge to book form, I spent hours interviewing him (on the bike and off) over the course of several years. Working with him also gave me the opportunity to attend numerous medical conferences on subjects like orthopedics and cardiology, thus giving this English major a substantial medical education.

Andy Pruitt is simply the most experienced and most expert bike fit authority in the U.S., if not the world. For 25 years, he has studied how the human body should sit on a bicycle for maximum comfort as well as to produce the most power.

In addition, he has ministered to thousands of cyclists—from riders like us to elite performers, including Tour de France champion Lance Armstrong.

There's no quirk of anatomy affecting bike fit that Andy hasn't seen. No fit-related cycling injury has passed him unnoticed.

Cycling is not an injury-prone sport. Unlike running, it's non-impact. Many riders go through whole careers with only minor aches and pains. But although cycling is generally easy on the body, things sometimes go wrong. Overuse, poor bike fit, badly designed training programs, crashes, aging—all can lead to injury.

Because of this, there's a saying in Boulder, Colorado: "You'll eventually have to see Andy." You can go early in the course of an injury and get it fixed quickly, or you can wait until it becomes chronic.

But one way or the other, many riders end up at the clinic Andy directs, the Boulder Center for Sports Medicine. They sit in a waiting room with walls festooned by bikes hanging on hooks and autographed jerseys of great riders, including Armstrong, Christian Vande Velde, Julie Furtado, Andrea Peron, Connie Carpenter and Dede Demet-Barry.

Andy helps lesser lights, too. I credit him for my own continued ability to ride.

In late 1994, I injured my knee skiing powder on a tree-covered slope. It didn't seem too bad and I skied the rest of the day. After all, lift tickets are expensive. But over the next month, the pain got worse and more debilitating.

That's when I went to Andy. He and his orthopedic associate at the time, James Holmes, M.D., performed an arthroscope.

They found damage to the articular cartilage on the end of my femur, the sort of injury that could eventually lead to a knee replacement, especially on a knee that had been previously injured in college football.

Here's where Andy and Jim's extensive experience with athletes saved the day.

Formerly there had been no good treatment options. But they knew about a relatively new procedure (in 1995) called micro-fracture. It worked, and I've been riding, hiking and even running pain-free ever since.

It was only several years later, after Andy was sure the procedure had been a success, that he told me the prognosis for this injury for people over 40 is quite poor. His skill helped me beat the odds.

What if you don't live near Colorado? Simply read this book and follow Andy's advice.

It just may save you a trip to Boulder.

PART 1
Bike Fit

Chapter 1
Bike Fit Rules

Cyclists are often obsessed with bike fit. The more experienced they become, the more they worry about the subtle differences that a couple of millimeters can make.

Eddy Merckx, probably the greatest cyclist who ever lived, carried a 5-mm allen key in his jersey pocket. He was famous for making slight adjustments in saddle height, often several times a day. Sometimes he raised or lowered his saddle while on the bike during races.

It's often said that Merckx was persnickety about bike fit because he suffered nagging pain from injuries in a crash. But he also had an undetected physical abnormality that gave him problems during his whole career.

A few years ago, Eddy brought his son Axel to my office. (Axel now rides for the Domo-Farm Frites team and is an excellent pro in his own right.) I examined the young rider and found a significant leg-length inequality, primarily in his femur.

Incredibly, Eddy has the same problem.

When I diagnosed this, Eddy knew why he had been so uncomfortable on the bike despite his great success. At the thought of all the pain he had suffered—pain that could have been alleviated with a properly shimmed and adjusted cleat—he remarked, with his characteristic rueful grin, "Where were you when I was riding?"

Merckx's constant fiddling with bike fit points up what all cyclists know. First, if you're uncomfortable, riding is no fun. And because bike fit is so closely allied to power production, no one wants to squander even one watt of hard-earned power due to a poor position on the bike.

Fortunately, it isn't hard to find your ideal riding position.

Rule 1: Bike fit is a marriage between bike and rider.

If the two are incompatible, the marriage will fail. Just as married couples must adjust to each other, so must a bike and rider.

There's an important qualifier to this analogy. The bike can be adjusted to the rider's anatomy in multiple ways, such as moving the saddle up or down or changing the stem. But the body can be adjusted only in minor ways—with a carefully designed stretching program and by adapting to progressively longer rides. So the second rule is:

Rule 2: Make the bike fit your body; don't make your body fit the bike.

It's easy to adjust the bike but difficult to stretch or contort your body into some pre-conceived "ideal" position.

If you have long legs coupled with a short torso and arms, your bike needs a relatively short top tube/stem combination (often called "reach"). If you have stubby legs and most of your height is in your torso, you need a long top tube and stem.

Forget what your favorite pro rider's bike looks like unless your body is a carbon copy of his. Make your bike look like you, not like your hero.

Rule 3: Dynamic bike fit is better than static bike fit.

Most bike fit systems are static. They are done with a rider sitting motionless on a trainer or from a set of formulas using body-part measurements. Static and numerical formulas are an important starting point, from which we can move to dynamic fit.

Reflective markers, videotape and a computer are used in our dynamic methods for pedaling analysis and precision bike fit.

A pedaling rider is constantly moving on the bike. As you pedal, you actually rise or levitate slightly from the saddle. So ideal saddle height is different when you're pedaling compared to when you're just sitting motionless.

At the Boulder Center for Sports Medicine, we use a dynamic system to determine bike fit variables such as saddle height.

First, we attach reflective markers to specific anatomical landmarks on the rider's knee, ankle and hip (photo). Then we put him on the trainer and have him pedal.

We videotape the pedaling rider. A computer converts him into a 3-D stick figure. From that data we can determine exact and functional fit features such as saddle height, saddle fore/aft position and reach to the handlebar.

Again, there's nothing wrong with static bike fit and mathematical formulas as a starting place. In fact, in this book I'll suggest a number of ways to find ballpark figures for these important measurements. For 95 percent of riders, this book's information will enable powerful and pain-free cycling.

But if you're constantly uncomfortable on the bike or beset with nagging injuries, there's no substitute for an anatomical dynamic bike fit done while you're actually pedaling.

Rule 4: Cycling is a sport of repetition.

At a cadence of 90 revolutions per minute, a 6-hour century ride requires 32,400 iterations of the pedal stroke for each leg. That's a lot of repetition!

Worse, each pedal stroke is almost identical—your knee tracks in the same plane when observed from the front, and it bends the same amount at the top of each stroke.

As a result, a minor misfit (for instance, the saddle too low by several millimeters or a leg-length inequality of 5 mm) can lead to major problems over time. That's why fit is so important.

Chapter 2
Saddle Position

Saddle position is the key fit variable and the most important measurement to get right.

A low saddle often leads to problems in the front of the knee because the knee is bent excessively at the top of the pedal stroke where power production begins. There's too much shearing force on the back of the *patella* (kneecap) where it tracks in a groove in the *femur* (thighbone).

A saddle set too high can cause pain behind the knee because you have to reach for the pedals, excessively stretching the hamstrings.

A high saddle also compromises power production. This is because the patella acts like a fulcrum in the leg's lever system. As the leg straightens, it's less effective until the patella loses contact with the femur entirely at a knee bend of about 15 degrees. Inappropriately high saddles mean you lose power because the patella is no longer an effective fulcrum.

A saddle also can be positioned by sliding it fore or aft along its rails on the seatpost. This is an important fit variable because it controls where you sit in relation to the bike's bottom bracket (center of crank rotation).

Finally, a saddle can be tilted up or down or be completely level.

Saddle Height: Road Bikes

To find a close approximation of your ideal saddle height, the simplest method is often the best:

With the bike on a trainer, pedal for five minutes in a medium gear until your muscles are loose and you're positioned on the saddle where you normally sit. Unclip and place both heels on the pedals.

Saddle height is correct when you can sit squarely, straighten your leg, and reach the pedal with your heel.

Pedal slowly. Your knees should reach full extension at the bottom of each stroke. Your heels should almost, but not quite, lose contact with the pedals as they go around the bottom (photo). Your pelvis should remain level with no hip rocking.

When you clip back into the pedals with the ball of your feet over the pedal axles, the length of your feet makes your legs longer. The result is the appropriate amount of knee bend at the bottom of the stroke.

The LeMond Method

Another commonly used method was popularized by three-time Tour de France winner Greg LeMond. It's an approach that Greg learned from his French coach, Cyrille Guimard.

In bare feet and wearing cycling shorts, stand with your back against a wall. Have your feet about six inches apart. Put a carpenter's square between your legs so that one side is flush against the wall. The other side should project in front of you from between your legs. (The idea is to have a measuring device that is level with the floor. A large thin book or record album—remember those?—can work, too.) Pull up on whatever you use until you feel pressure against your crotch equal to what a saddle produces when you're pedaling easily.

Have someone measure from the top of the horizontal edge of the carpenter's square to the floor. Record this crotch-to-floor distance precisely in centimeters. Saddle height, as measured from the center of the bottom bracket axle to the top of the saddle along the seat tube, should equal 0.883 times your crotch-to-floor distance. For instance, if your crotch-to-floor measurement is 87 cm, your saddle height is 0.883 x 87 or 76.8 cm.

There are five important qualifiers to this formula:

- It was developed in the early 1980s when equipment was different. Cycling shoes had thicker soles, and pedals with toe clips positioned the foot higher above the axle than modern clipless pedals do. These factors mean that the 0.883 multiplier may be too high when you're using modern equipment. Still, it's a good starting point for ballparking saddle height.

- Riders with long feet for their height may find that this formula produces a saddle that's too low. Long feet have the effect of lengthening legs beyond standard proportions.

- Cyclists with excessive soft tissue over their sit bones may find the saddle too low. After sitting on it for a while, the soft tissue compresses.

- Adding thickness to your shoes—in the form of insoles or cycling orthotics that extend under the ball of the foot—has the effect of lengthening your legs. This requires a higher saddle.

- Adding thickness between your crotch and the saddle, like when you wear thick winter cycling tights, effectively shortens your legs and requires a slightly lower saddle.

Saddle Height: Mountain Bikes

Determine saddle height for a mountain bike using the road bike guidelines.

There's one exception. If your ATB's crankarms are longer than your road bike's, you should lower the saddle an amount equal to the difference in crankarm length. This is necessary to give you the correct amount of bend in your knee at the bottom of the stroke.

For example, if you run 170-mm crankarms on your road bike but 175-mm on your mountain bike, lower your mountain bike's saddle 5 mm.

Frame Size

LeMond's crotch-to-floor measurement will help you find your frame size, too.

Simply multiply your measurement by 0.65. For example, if your crotch-to-floor distance is 87 cm, then 87 x 0.65 = 56.5 cm. This means you should ride a frame that measures 56 to 57 cm from the center of the bottom bracket to the top of the top tube, measured along the seat tube.

However, many current frames don't have the traditional diamond shape with a top tube parallel to the ground. It's hard to find their center-to-top measurement. Most manufacturers give a "virtual seat tube height" measurement when their bikes are designed with angled top tubes. This makes it easier to get the correct frame size.

Some riders need a larger frame than this method suggests.

For example, if you need your handlebar fairly high compared to the saddle, you may want to use 0.7 as a multiplier. The same holds if you have a relatively long torso or arms and need a frame with a longer top tube. As seat tubes lengthen, so do top tubes.

Saddle Setback

This important measurement involves the fore/aft location of the saddle and is contingent on the length of your *femur* (thighbone). It has nothing to do with a frame's seat tube angle.

The saddle setback should put your knee's center of rotation directly over the pedal axle of the forward crankarm when it's horizontal.

Correct setback is important for two reasons:

1. It positions your knee so that your power can be driven directly into the pedal at the point in the crank circle where it does the most good.

2. It means that your hips are neither too far forward nor too far behind the bottom bracket. Either of these extremes can cause injury or chronic pain as you pedal.

The center of the knee's rotation must be directly over the ball of the foot (and therefore the center of the pedal axle) at the time of maximum power production. Of course, some riders may not have their cleats directly under the ball of their feet (I'll discuss this later), but this rule holds for everyone else.

To determine saddle setback, you need a plumb line that you can make from a piece of string with a heavy washer or nut tied to one end. You also need a friend to help.

1. Put your bike on a trainer. If the surface isn't level, shim the trainer's legs until it is. Pedal for five minutes to warm up and find the place on the saddle where you normally ride.

2. Stop pedaling so the crankarms are horizontal (parallel to the floor) and your right foot is for-

ward. Take care that you don't raise or lower your heel when you stop pedaling. Have your friend watch to be sure it's in the same position as when you're turning the crank.

When determining saddle setback, drop the plumb line from the front of the knee. It's an easier anatomical landmark to find than the traditional "bump below the knee" (tibial tuberosity).

3. Your friend should drop the plumb line from the front of your right leg's kneecap (photo). The line should touch the end of the crankarm. If the line is in front or behind the end, loosen the seatpost bolts and slide the saddle forward or backward on the rails to get it right.

4. Pedal for a minute to re-establish your normal position on the saddle, then recheck with the plumb line and readjust the setback, if necessary. Keep at it until you get it right. Be patient— this is an important measurement.

5. Now check the left leg. If the line doesn't touch the end of the crankarm like on the right side, it means you might have an inequality in femur length. If so, adjust the saddle setback to split the difference.

Changing the saddle's fore/aft position can change its height. If you had to slide the saddle a considerable distance to achieve proper setback, recheck saddle height. If it needs to be changed, do it and then recheck setback.

Some authorities say that the plumb line should be dropped from the bony bump below your kneecap (called the *tibial tuberosity*). The line should then bisect the pedal axle when setback is right.

I prefer to use the front of the kneecap because it's an easier anatomical landmark to find. Also, the bony bump varies in thickness and location among individuals, making it less precise.

Finally, it's easier to see if the plumb line touches the end of the crankarm than it is to judge its relationship to the pedal axle. The end results are very close.

CAUTION! **It's a fashion statement in some cycling circles to have the saddle jammed as far back on the seatpost as possible so the rider can sport**

what he considers a "pro" position. But this set-back is right only for riders with long femurs coupled with a flexible low back and hamstrings.

EXAMPLE Greg LeMond has extremely long fe-murs. His kneecaps seem to be only slightly above his ankles! So for him, a bike with a slack seat tube angle, a long top tube and the saddle jammed all the way back is appropriate. Such a position puts his knee over the pedal axle or just slightly behind it.

But most people aren't built Greg's way. For-mer pro Ron Kiefel, a seven-time Tour de France competitor, once moved his saddle back when a famous rider he admired told him he'd be faster if he did. Ron didn't get faster. Instead, he developed severe back pain and missed several weeks of rac-ing.

The moral of this story: Let your femur length, not your hero, determine your saddle position.

Saddle Tilt

When I go to mass-participation cycling events like centuries or Ride the Rockies, I'm amazed at the varia-tions in saddle tilt. Some riders have the nose pointed down at extreme angles—as much as 30 degrees. Other riders tilt the nose so high that their saddle looks like a jumbo jet taking off. It's painful to look at. Here's the rule:

- If you're a recreational or touring cyclist and you have the nose of your saddle pointing up or down, your bike doesn't fit. It's probably the reach to the handlebar (see below) that's incor-rect.

Other points:

- In general, your saddle should be positioned level with the ground. It should not be angled up or down. Check with a carpenter's level or a yardstick placed lengthwise on the saddle and compared to something horizontal like a tabletop or windowsill.

- If the nose of the saddle is down, you'll have too much weight on your arms and hands as you try to stop sliding forward. The result may be arm fatigue and numbness in your fingers.

- Downward sloping saddles also put too much of your weight on the front wheel. This degrades bike handling.

- Tilting the saddle down doesn't solve crotch problems like numbness or excessive saddle sores. Instead, it can make them worse. When you're constantly sliding down the saddle and then pushing yourself back, crotch irritation results.

- If the nose of the saddle points up, it will push against the soft tissue, blood vessels and nerves in your crotch. This leads to saddle sores, numbness and the risk of erection difficulties (for males).

- When the nose points up, it also has ramifications for the lower back. The normal curvature is changed, often resulting in pain.

Despite these risks, there are two exceptions to the level-saddle rule:

1. People with unusual pelvic tilts or lumbar postures (swayback, for instance) sometimes

require a slight upward tilt (1 to 3 degrees) so they can get their weight on their sit bones rather than on soft tissue. Posture irregularities don't have to be so pronounced that people notice. For example, you could have a very subtle swayback syndrome that tilts your pelvis forward as you lean over to hold the handlebar. But usually a simple adjustment—raising the handlebar slightly—will let you level the saddle and still get the pressure off the pudendal nerves in your crotch.

2. In rare instances, the saddle should be tilted down slightly. This is appropriate mainly when in a low time trial position with aero bars.

Chapter 3
Handlebar Position

Reach is the combination of top tube and stem length with some input from saddle fore/aft position.

Reach to the handlebar determines the angle of your torso in relation to the ground. The shorter the reach, the greater the angle. Tourists sit relatively upright while time trialists want their backs to be almost parallel to the ground. Your best torso angle will depend on the way you ride, your goals in cycling, your body's limitations and your comfort.

Other contributors to reach are the type of brake levers you have and the handlebar shape. Some bars are longer from front to back, enlarging the reach. Some have a deeper drop. The shape of the levers' bend can affect where you grip the lever hoods, changing the reach.

Reach is the most individual part of bike fit. It depends on a wide range of factors including hamstring and low-back flexibility, low-back strength, posture, arm and torso length, and shoulder strength.

Each of these factors also plays a role in the height of the bar in relation to the saddle.

Age is part of the equation, too. As we get older, we often lose flexibility regardless of how much stretching we do. The handlebar has to come up, and often the reach must be reduced.

In the days of conventional quill stems and threaded steerer tubes, adjusting handlebar height was relatively easy—just raise the stem. But with the acceptance of threadless headsets, handlebar height adjustments are more complicated.

TIP If you're considering a new or custom bike, don't let the shop cut the steerer tube until you're sure the fit is right.

Reach to a Drop Bar

Use the following advice to approximate correct reach to the handlebar and set your saddle/handlebar height differential. This advice is for a drop (downturned) road handlebar unless otherwise noted.

CAUTION! Be sure your saddle height and setback are correct before you adjust the handlebar.

These are only guidelines, but they're useful starting points:

- An old Italian wives' tale says to determine reach, put your elbow against the tip of the saddle and extend your open hand toward the handlebar. The end of your middle finger should come within an inch or so of the bar.

- To get a ballpark figure for the relationship of handlebar height to saddle height, measure your fist across the knuckles from little finger to index finger. Then use a stem height that makes the difference between the bar top and saddle top equal to your fist measurement. Take several rides, then make adjustments based on feedback from your body.

CAUTION! These anatomical approximations assume that all of your body parts are in proportion. Is there a relationship between the size of your fist and the length of your upper body? Or the flexibility of your low back? Sometimes—and sometimes not. Still, these approximations are a useable starting point.

Another formula says that your reach to the handlebar should be such that 40 percent of your weight is on the front wheel and 60 percent on the rear. There's no good way to determine those percentages, however.

One suggestion is to put the bike's rear wheel on one bathroom scale and the front wheel on another. Then sit on the bike and see if 40 percent of the combined weight registers on the front scale. This is a rough approach at best because it's done while you're stationary rather than pedaling.

CAUTION! Flexibility matters. If you can't stand with locked knees and bend over to touch your toes after only a minimal warmup, none of the static bike fit formulas will work for you. None of them! You'll need a higher handlebar, set closer to the saddle.

EXAMPLE At the Boulder Center for Sports Medicine, we recently diagnosed a young pro with a congenital back ailment. He has since raised his handlebar almost 3 inches. He went from a 12-cm bar/saddle differential to about 5 cm. He still looks like a pro on the bike and he's amazed at the increased comfort.

Bike shops fit customers to bikes. In good shops, the employees have extensive training and experience. But because of all the variables, it's beyond even the best bike fitter's skills to get reach right on the first try. This dimension is just too personal.

As a result, shop employees shouldn't be upset when customers come back and want a stem change after they've ridden several hundred miles. Still, I've heard shop people complain: "I spent two hours fitting this guy, and he had the nerve to come back and want a different stem!"

You bet he had the nerve—literally. The nerves in his hands or neck hurt after he'd ridden several hours. Something wasn't right. It's a precarious balance and bike shops need to realize this.

Reach to a Flat Handlebar

Some road riders like to install a flat bar, especially on a commuting bike so they can sit upright on busy streets. It's easy to duplicate your drop-bar reach when you convert to a flat bar, or if you want to set up a mountain bike.

1. Put some blue carpenter's chalk on the web between your thumb and index finger.

2. Pedal your properly adjusted road bike on the trainer for several minutes, then measure the distance from the tip of the saddle to the blue chalk mark you left on the brake hoods.

3. Without washing your hands, ride your bike with the flat bar and note where the blue mark appears on the grips.

4. The distance from the tip of the saddle to the chalk marks should be the same on both bikes.

Handlebar Width

Handlebars come in several widths. Some manufacturers measure drop bars from the center of the bar ends, while others measure from the outside of these openings. Generally, the bar on your road bike should equal the width of your shoulders (photo).

A handlebar width that's equal to shoulder width provides support and control while giving lungs room to expand.

To determine your shoulder width, have a friend measure from one *acromio-clavicular joint* to another.

The A-C joint is the prominent bump on top and about two inches from the outside of each shoulder (p. 86). If the distance is 42 cm, that's the width of the bar to use.

Criterium specialists may prefer a narrower bar so they can squeeze through tiny openings in the pack.

Distance riders usually like wider bars for more comfort and steering stability. Wider bars aren't a panacea, however, because they can create their own set of physical problems. Women usually have narrower shoulders and less upper-body strength to help them cope with ill-fitting bars.

Brake Lever Placement

A drop bar should be nearly level when looked at from the side. This will be the case if the bar is positioned so the flat lower portion points to the bike's rear brake.

Once the bar is set, position the brake levers:

1. Hold a straightedge under the flat part of the drop so that it projects forward (photo).

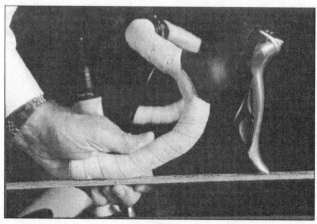

The brake lever tip should touch a straightedge held flat against the drop.

2. Move the lever on the bar till the tip just touches.

3. Anatomical handlebars with flat sections in the bends for hand comfort may affect step 2. If you have this type of bar, go with this general rule: You should be able to reach the levers equally well when your hands are atop the hoods or in the drops.

Touring or long distance cyclists may want to rotate the bar in the stem so the drops point at the rear hub rather than the brake. This raises the top of the lever hoods, putting them closer to the saddle to create a more upright position.

Compared to Campagnolo brake levers, Shimano models have a more abrupt transition from the lever body to the handlebar. Some riders find one brand or the other to be more comfortable.

If you're updating from brake-only levers to combination brake/shift levers, remember that the new levers have bodies about 1 cm longer to accommodate all the internal mechanisms. As a result, you need a stem 1 cm shorter.

It's fine to position one brake lever slightly different than the other. Remember, the bike should look like you.

For example, some riders have one arm that's slightly shorter than the other thanks to a broken bone or congenital factors. A broken collarbone can cause the same effect. In these cases, you'll want to have the brake lever higher on the short-arm side.

TIP **One signal that you need an asymmetrical reach is a stabbing pain behind one shoulder blade or on one side of your neck. Check by riding a trainer. Have a friend look from the front and from behind to see if your shoulders are level. Adjust your brake levers until they are.**

Hand Positions on Drop Bar

The shape of drop handlebars has remained basically the same for a hundred years. There's good reason for this apparent lack of innovation—the standard down-turned shape is best suited for comfort and control. It provides a number of hand positions, too. This is crucial because leaving your hands in one place guarantees numb and tingling fingers.

TIP Your wrist should be in a neutral, handshake position as much as possible. If your wrist angles toward the thumb or little finger, you'll experience numbing nerve pressure.

There are three primary hand positions on a drop handlebar:

1. On the lever hoods. Place the web of your hand atop the brake lever hood with the thumb to the inside and the four fingers to the outside. Curl your index finger across the top of the lever. Be sure your wrist is straight. From this position, it's easy to brake with one or two fingers and shift if you have combined brake/shift levers. This is also the standard position for out-of-saddle climbing.

One useful variation on this position (assuming you have levers with concealed cables) is to put the middle of your palm on the tip of the hood as if you were resting your hand on the end of a cane. This stretches you out slightly and aids aerodynamics. When the reach is correct, your forearms will rest on the top of the handlebar. You'll feel improved support, comfort and aero-dynamics.

CAUTION! You may see some roadies try to get more aero by resting their forearms on top of the bar. They grasp the cable coming from the side of each Shimano brake/shift lever. This is extremely dangerous! The cables provide only a flimsy grip, so hitting a bump can cause loss of control and a nasty crash.

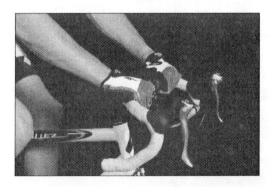

2. On the tops near the stem. Place both hands, palms down, on the bar beside the stem. Some riders prefer to move farther out, near where the bar begins to curve forward, for added stability.

This is the standard climbing position. It allows you to sit more upright for added power and easier breathing. Many riders also use it for easy cruising because of the upright position.

If you need to ride one-handed (while drinking from your bottle, for instance), hold the bar with the other hand near the stem. If you hit a bump or are jostled from the side, you're less likely to swerve. This works because the closer to the bar you put your hand, the less leverage you have for steering. A bump isn't likely to make you jerk the bar.

CAUTION! **You'll sometimes see a racer reach back to grab a teammate's hand and sling him forward on a climb or into a better position for a sprint. They'll hold their bars near the stem for better stability. Don't try this move unless you know exactly what you're doing. It's an easy way to tangle the bikes and take your friend down with you.**

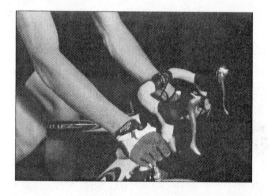

3. On the drops. Grip the bar's low section near the curves ("hooks") for descending or fast, flat riding. This is the most aerodynamic position on a drop handlebar. It also produces the most powerful braking because you can pull on the levers with several fingers while opposing the force with your thumb wrapped around the bar.

Some riders defy conventional wisdom and grip the drops during out-of-saddle climbing. They argue that this provides more leverage to let them get their upper body into the pedal stroke.

Climbing in the drops used to be discouraged on the grounds that the bent-over posture makes breathing difficult and aerodynamics doesn't matter going uphill. But now that top climbers like Marco Pantani are seen on the drops more often than not, more riders are trying it. And they do seem to be going faster.

TIP **No matter which grip you use, remember to change it frequently. If your bike fits properly, holding the bar tops will be as comfortable as riding in the drops. If you are comfortable only with your hands in one location, it's a sign that your reach to the handlebar is incorrect.**

CAUTION! **Some riders install a long stem with the bar much lower than the saddle. They think this makes them look like a pro. But the reach is often so excessive that they have to ride most of the time on the tops with their hands next to the stem. Then they have to move their hands each time they want to brake or shift.**

Modern brake/shift levers are designed to reward riding with the hands on the lever hoods, where both shifting and braking are readily accessible. This is, to use a computer term, the default position. Still, you need to change your grip every few minutes to avoid hand numbness.

Aero Bar Position

Aero bars can be attached to most drop handlebars. They aid comfort and improve aerodynamic efficiency. But they also can be quite dangerous if you use them in a group or paceline. Your bike control isn't as sharp, and your hands are a long way from the brake levers.

As a result, there are only two reasons to install aero bars on your road bike:

- For long-distance cycling when many miles are ridden solo or with just a couple of other riders. Install the aero bars so when you're on them, a plumb line dropped from the front of your shoulder exits at the back of your elbow (photo). In other words, your upper arm should be fairly vertical with the elbow just ahead of the shoulder.

A balanced, comfortable aero-bar position has the elbows just ahead of the shoulders.

- For time trialing when getting low is less important than getting narrow. Adjust the armrests so your arms are within the width of your hips when viewed from the front. Use a mirror or have a friend check. Also, slide the saddle forward 1-2 cm depending on comfort and power production.

A pure time trialing position has a plumb line from the front of the forward knee falling 2 cm in front of the end of the crankarm when it's horizontal. Adjust the saddle's fore/aft position and its height, then adjust the aero bars as just described.

Chapter 4
Pedals and Cleats

Modern clipless pedals are a significant innovation compared to the clips, straps and slotted cleats of just a few years ago.

With clipless pedals, there's no pressure from toe straps across the instep or from toe clips digging into the end of your toes. Clipless pedals are easy to enter and exit. In a crash, your feet automatically disengage so you aren't attached to the bike as you fall.

Clipless pedal systems have, however, made bike fit more important.

With slotted cleats, if one leg was slightly longer than the other, the short leg's cleat would rise slightly off the pedal rail at the bottom of the stroke. This compensated for the inequality. The slight play in toe straps, even when pulled fairly tight, also helped.

But with clipless pedals, your foot is locked in and no compensation is possible. Over many repetitions of the pedal stroke, this can lead to problems such as low-back pain.

Also, the first clipless pedals didn't have *float*, the ability to let the foot rotate a few degrees outward or inward as you pedal. (Slotted cleats wore with time, so they allowed float even though it wasn't intended.) Today, nearly all clipless pedals permit float. This has lessened the injuries that were associated with the original rigid models.

Still, adjusting pedals and cleats is supremely important. Rotationally, you need to find the center, neutral position for each foot so you have float both inward and outward. And you need to find the correct fore/aft location over the pedal axle. Here's how.

Fore/aft Foot Position

For many riders, cleat position is correct when the ball of the foot is centered over the pedal axle.

In general, the ball of your foot should be directly over the centerline of the pedal axle (photo). Here are pointers for obtaining this so-called "neutral" position.

- The ball of the foot is the first *metatarsal phalange joint*—directly behind the big toe. Feel it with your finger, then mark the side of your shoe. Align the mark with the center of the pedal axle. Slide your cleats forward or back until you get it right.

- This placement works best for men's size 9 feet (Euro size 41-42). Riders with longer feet will do well to move the cleats rearward on the shoe to put more of the foot in front of the pedal axle. In contrast, riders with shorter feet may move their cleats toward the front of the shoe so they are pedaling more "on their toes." The reason is that longer feet want stability and shorter feet want more lever length.

- Your shoe model will determine where your cleats can be placed. Each shoe manufacturer drills the same hole pattern for several sizes. If you're at the extremes for the hole pattern (because you have long or short feet), it may limit your ability to put the cleats in the best position.

- Long-distance riders often find that they can avoid painful numbness and "hot foot" by sliding their cleats all the way back. This puts the ball of their feet as far ahead of direct pedal pressure as possible. In fact, some ultramarathon riders go so far as to drill the shoe soles so they can move their cleats even farther to the rear. (For another solution to the hot foot problem, see the section on *metatarsal buttons*.)

EXAMPLE Race Across America legend Lon Haldeman's business is taking riders across the U.S. on his PAC Tours—rapid, three-week transcontinental rides that average between 110 and 140 miles per day

Sometimes a rider will develop such extreme foot discomfort that it's hard to continue. When this happens, Haldeman has a time-tested solution. He drills their shoes and moves their cleats as much as 2 cm farther back. This usually provides an instant cure, with pain-free pedaling the rest of the tour.

Many ultramarathon riders claim that this modification doesn't diminish the power or suppleness of their pedal stroke, so they ride with their cleats rearward all the time. However, this contention has yet to be tested in the lab.

CAUTION! Drilling shoe soles should be a last resort. Don't try it until you've exhausted the other "hot foot" remedies in this book. Drilling can ruin expensive shoes unless you know exactly what you're doing. Putting additional holes in some soles can weaken them. Also, moving cleats far to the rear may reduce "hot foot" symptoms but create other physical problems as the body copes with the extreme change in position.

Rotational Cleat Position

In addition to the fore/aft setting, cleats can be rotated to accommodate foot postures that point in or out from the centerline of the bike. Even with pedals that provide some amount of free rotation (*float*), it's important to set your cleats properly.

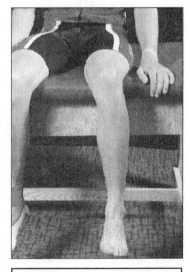

The goal is for your feet to automatically be in the center of the cleat's rotational arc, no matter what angle they naturally assume. This allows them to move one way or another from your "neutral" center.

Sit like this to determine the natural angle of your feet for mounting cleats.

To find the correct angle to mount your cleats, sit on the edge of a table or counter and let your feet dangle (photo). Your hips, knees and ankles should all be at 90-degree angles. Let your feet hang where they want to—don't force them to toe in or out. Just accept what you get. But remember to keep your ankles flexed at 90 degrees.

Now look down to see the angles your feet are making. Those are the angles you want to reproduce when you set your cleats. Have someone help you by looking at your feet dangling off the table and again when you mount the cleats and sit on the bike.

Two caveats:

- Most people's feet don't toe in or out at the same angle. Be prepared to set your cleats at different angles depending on how each foot behaves.

- When some people bend forward, the angle of their feet changes due to internal rotation at the hips. So, bend forward on the table the same amount you do to reach the handlebar on your bike. If your foot angle changes, use the angle created when you lean forward.

Forefoot Varus

As many as 87 percent of all feet have *forefoot varus*. Varus is when the ball of the foot at mid stance is raised off a level plane for your normal walking gait.

In cycling, varus causes us to internally rotate the shin (illustration, p. 40). This, in turn, drives the knee toward the top tube. The result is a significant loss of power, and it's the most common cause of anterior medial knee injuries

Forefoot varus can be neutralized by custom orthotics, wedges made by Bicycle Fitting Systems, Inc., and anatomic shoes such as the Body Geometry models from Specialized.

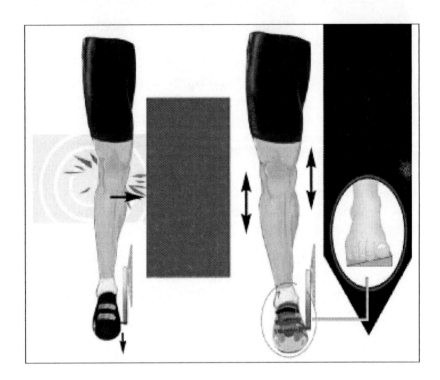

Uncorrected forefoot varus (left) can injure knees and steal pedaling power. The solution (right) is to use shoes, orthotics or other devices that neutralize varus. *(Courtesy of Specialized)*

Pedal Float

Most riders get along fine with only 3 to 6 degrees of rotation by the cleat before it snaps free from the pedal. On rare occasions, a rider might need a pedal system that provides more than 9 degrees.

The less float you have, the more power you can produce because your leg muscles aren't working so hard to stabilize your foot rotationally on the pedal.

There's an endpoint to the transfer of power to the pedal (much like in walking). Some extremely duck-footed riders need pedals with more float but only so they can achieve their normal foot posture on the pedal.

Of course, your anklebones shouldn't hit the crank-arms and your heels shouldn't hit the chainstays. If they do, you need orthotic arch supports and/or fore-foot varus correction.

Riders with unstable feet would bang their ankle-bones frequently on old-fashioned straight crankarms, especially when trying to put out lots of power while seated on short hills. Modern crankarms that curve or angle away from narrow bottom brackets all but elimi-nate this problem.

PART 2

Remedies for Cycling Injuries

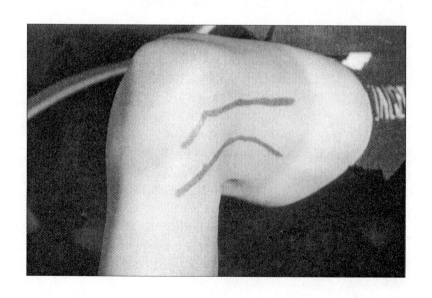

Chapter 5
Knees

Cycling should be hard on the knees.

At an average cadence of 90 rpm, a recreational rider churns out 5,400 pedal revolutions per hour, or about 1.5 million pedal strokes while racking up a 5,000-mile year. A pro racer, logging a typical season of training and competition, will push the pedals around an astounding 7.5 million times. Much of this knee movement is against firm resistance.

And yet cycling is relatively benign for this complex joint because there's no heel strike as there is in running. In fact, bike riding is the rehabilitation of choice for most knee injuries. Even if you can't walk, run or limp around the block on crutches, you can ride a bike.

The reason is that cycling isn't a full weight-bearing activity. The pedals are always descending away from you so your knees can operate without excessive stress. Injured knees, knees that have been surgically repaired, and aging knees all want movement—and you want exercise. It all comes together on a bike.

Occasionally, however, cyclists' knees do become injured. After all, that's one hard-working joint! But most knee problems respond quickly to treatment.

This chapter will take you through the list of common cycling-related knee injuries and tell you what to do about them. In most cases, core treatment consists of two key components:

- Icing
- Use of a NSAID, medication that relieves pain and reduces inflammation

How to Ice Injuries

In general for injuries where icing is appropriate, apply ice as many as three times a day for 15 to 20 minutes each time.

I frequently recommend icing injuries in this book. Here's how to do it. I won't repeat this advice in subsequent pages, so check back here to recall the proper procedure.

- Put crushed ice or small ice cubes in a plastic zip-shut food storage bag. Place cloth (a washcloth works well) on the skin over the injury. Lay the ice bag on top and hold it in place with an elastic bandage. Don't fasten the bandage too tightly or it will increase the cold on your skin and might cause damage.

- Keep the ice pack in place for 15-20 minutes, remove it for 20-30 minutes, and reapply. Repeat the process as often as three times a day.

TIP **Some injuries respond to *focal icing*—rubbing ice directly on the exact spot of the pain. Fill a small paper cup nearly full with water and put it in the freezer overnight. Gently massage the afflicted area with the exposed end of the ice, like you're rubbing it with an ice cream cone. As the ice melts, peel the paper cup away to expose more ice.**

Put a towel under the injury to absorb the melting ice. Stop when your skin begins to get numb. Several five-minute sessions per hour up to three times a day should provide plenty of therapy for your ailment without injuring your skin.

Here's a related technique you can try for an inflamed tendon. First, ice the area. Then perform *cross-*

friction massage. This is done by rubbing across the tendon fibers with your thumb for about 10 minutes. Then reapply ice. Cross-friction massage may make the pain worse in the short term, but improvement quickly follows.

EXAMPLE **A member of the U.S. Cycling Team with a bad case of patellar tendinitis had to fly to South America for a stage race. He didn't think he would be able to compete. I instructed him to perform icing and cross-friction massage on the plane. He was ready to race after two days of travel and self-treatment.**

How to Use a NSAID

In the same way that icing is a frequent fix for cycling injuries, so is the use of a non-steroidal anti-inflammatory drug (NSAID). Common trade names are Aleve, Motrin and Advil. Most drug stores offer house brands at a substantial discount.

CAUTION! **Although NSAIDs are over-the-counter medications, their use can be dangerous. *Please obey the manufacturer's directions.* In particular, excessive doses combined with dehydration can lead to serious kidney problems in susceptible individuals.**

When using NSAIDs, you need to be especially careful on a tour or in periods of heavy training. Particularly in hot summer weather, these are situations when you might become chronically dehydrated. If this happens, NSAID use should be limited.

NSAIDs can be tough on your stomach lining, so reduce the risk by taking them with food.

Patellar Tendinitis

DESCRIPTION

Tendinitis is inflammation of a tendon, usually from overuse. In an inflammation, microscopic tears heal and become microscopic scars. The tearing and scarring cause an enlargement in the tendon, producing an increase in friction as the tendon moves. Pain results.

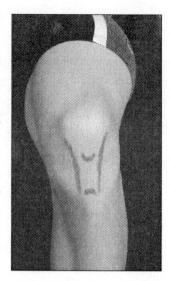

The patella in *patellar tendinitis* is the kneecap. It's surrounded by the tendon structure that connects the thigh's quadriceps muscle group to the lower leg.

SYMPTOMS

- You feel pain in the front of the knee, below the patella, when you pedal or walk upstairs. It'll probably be even worse descending stairs. It also hurts when you merely touch the tendon. There may be some swelling.

- The tendon might squeak like a rusty hinge when you bend your knee. This worrisome noise is called *crepitus* and means that the tendon's normal lubrication is in short supply.

- Your patella is a triangle. If you look down at it, the pain is usually centered on the lower tip (*inferior pole*) where it connects to the tendon. If the tendinitis is severe, you may get localized swelling. It will look like a little grape at the end of your patella.

CAUSES

- This injury often appears after hard sprinting, big-gear climbing or off-bike jumping activities. It also can occur after hard leg presses or squats.

- Simply doing too much, too soon.

TREATMENT

- Apply ice as many as three times a day for 15-20 minutes each time.

- Take a non-steroidal anti-inflammatory drug (NSAID) with food.

- Check your saddle height.

- Pedal easily or stop riding for several days.

Spring Knee

DESCRIPTION

This is another form of tendinitis that often strikes the complex of tendons in the front of the knee. It's an overuse injury that often starts in the early season, which gives it its name.

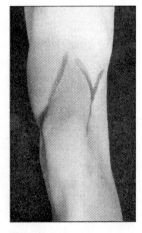

But it's not just a matter of too many early-season miles. It's typically the combination of riding, weight training and other activities that enthusiastic cyclists do in the spring.

SYMPTOMS

- You feel a sharp pain along the top of the patella, which is triangle-shaped with the point at the bottom. The pain usually occurs on the inner (*medial*) or outer (*lateral*) points on top, though it can appear anywhere around the kneecap.

- In rare cases, spring knee manifests itself as a tender spot two to three inches above the knee where tendon and muscle come together.

CAUSES

- Spring knee is associated with a combination of activities that cyclists often do during the early season: leg exercises such as squats or leg presses, increased mileage on the bike and perhaps downhill skiing—all in conjunction with cold weather that irritates tendons.

- You are predisposed to developing this injury when you have enough fitness to work out hard, but it's not cycling-specific fitness.

TREATMENT

- Apply ice as many as three times a day for 15-20 minutes each time.

- Take a non-steroidal anti-inflammatory drug (NSAID) with food.

- Check your saddle height.

- Pedal easily or stop riding for several days.

IF TENDINITIS REMEDIES DON'T WORK

- Find the error in your training or position that led to the injury. If you rode too few miles before a long tour or hard ride, don't make the mistake again. Revise your training plan so you gradually build your mileage.

- For bike fit problems that can hurt knees—including cleat position and saddle height—see the fitting instructions in this book. If you're still having trouble, get a professional bike fit from a certified coach, a reputable bike shop or a cycling-savvy facility such as the Boulder Center for Sports Medicine.

- If pain persists, a physical therapist might try *phonophoresis*, using ultra sound to drive a cortisone cream into the afflicted area.

- Injected cortisone is definitely *not* recommended due to possible long-term complications.

RETURNING TO RIDING AFTER TENDINITIS

When tendinitis pain has eased, use these tips as you get back on the bike:

- Before riding, apply a *counter-irritant* to increase blood to flow to the area. Use a commercial product (such as Icy Hot) or make your own by mixing baby oil and oil of wintergreen. Then shield the injured knee from cool wind with leg warmers or a light coating of petroleum jelly.

- Increase your cadence and reduce pedaling resistance by using lower gears.

- Raise your saddle about 3 mm.

- Always wear leg warmers or tights if the temperature is below 65 degrees F.

Chondromalacia

DESCRIPTION

Chondromalacia ranges from irritation of the *articular cartilage* on the back of the *patella* (kneecap) to actual degeneration that can lead to arthritis.

SYMPTOMS

- Pain behind the patella, often when climbing or descending stairs or pushing big gears.
- There might be audible clicking or grating.
- Aching and stiffness after sitting.

CAUSES

- Too much kneeling or squatting.
- Excessive use of big gears and a slow cadence.
- Weight training activities such as leg extensions that isolate and load the patella.
- Malalignment of the patella. The cartilage on the back of the kneecap can be roughened until it loses its normal glossy surface, resulting in irritation and pain. Like the tires on a car that's out of alignment, the kneecap can wear unevenly.

TREATMENT

- Apply ice as many as three times a day for 15-20 minutes each time.
- Take a non-steroidal anti-inflammatory drug (NSAID) with food.
- Cycling is generally good for chondromalacia because knees like smooth circles. The saddle should be set high because the lower the sad-

dle, the more shearing force on the back of the kneecap. Raise the saddle until your hips begin rocking during the pedal stroke, then lower it just enough to stop this motion.

TIP **Any time you raise the saddle, also raise the stem the same amount. Then you'll retain your ideal differential between the height of the handlebar and the top of the saddle.**

- Ride with a high cadence and low gears so there's little resistance on each pedal stroke. Avoid climbing, especially in the saddle.

IF THESE REMEDIES DON'T WORK

- Chondromalacia treatment has become a real art and includes the McConnell theory of strengthening the *vastus medialis* (the pear-shaped part of the quadriceps muscle just above and to the inner side of your knee). Your therapist should prescribe short-arc leg extensions and straight-leg raises, as well as cycling.

- Long-term relief from chondromalacia comes from developing a high level of vastus medialis strength combined with *gluteal* (butt muscle) strength.

- Some therapists tape the patella and surrounding area, although this is a temporary treatment.

When chondromalacia sufferers can walk downstairs pain-free after therapy, they usually have the symptoms under control.

Ilio-tibial Band Friction Syndrome

DESCRIPTION

The *ilio-tibial (IT) band* is a wide sheath of fibrous connective tissue extending from the crest of the hipbone to just below the knee along the outer side of the thigh.

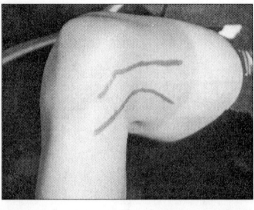

The band's lower end crosses the bony protuberance on the outer side of the knee. There is a *bursa* (fluid-filled sack) located between the bone and the IT band for protection and lubrication. In some situations, this area can be irritated. IT band syndrome is not only an inflammation of the tissue, it's also *bursitis*.

SYMPTOMS

- A sharp, stabbing pain on the outside, middle of the knee. It usually begins as a mild twinge, then increases until it feels like someone is tightening a hose clamp or stabbing you with an ice pick.

- The pain is usually worse during the power portion of the pedal stroke. Maximum friction occurs between the stroke's midpoint and bottom dead center.

CAUSES

- A stance on the bike that's too narrow.

- Badly positioned cleats. Usually they're too toed-in, but this isn't always the case.

- Biomechanical factors like "bowlegs."

- A saddle that's too high.

- Too much riding too soon. IT problems rarely happen after a period of base mileage.

- Flat feet and non-floating pedals are two other contributors.

TREATMENT

- Apply ice as many as three times a day for 10-15 minutes each time

- Take a non-steroidal anti-inflammatory drug (NSAID) with food.

- Widen your stance on the bike by moving your cleats as far to the inside of the shoe sole as possible. Or, put a washer on the pedal axle so the pedal doesn't thread as far into the crank-arm. Limit washer thickness to 2 mm so enough pedal screws in for safety. Some road riders install a triple crankset on their bike to take advantage of the longer bottom bracket axle.

- If your pedals don't have "float," it may help to position your cleats so your feet angle out more than normal.

- Lower your saddle about 6 mm. (IT band friction syndrome is one of the few knee problems where the saddle should be lowered rather than raised.)

- Over-the-counter arch supports or custom orthotics are often helpful because controlling the arch controls excessive *tibial* (lower leg) rotation. For this reason, anatomic shoes, such as the

Body Geometry models by Specialized, are effective.

CAUTION! **If these treatments don't relieve the pain in one day, stop riding but continue icing and NSAIDs. Once IT band friction syndrome gets established, it's hard to correct.**

IF THESE REMEDIES DON'T WORK

- You need to do specific stretches, such as the OBER stretch, on a regular basis. Learn them from a qualified physical therapist.

- Another possibility—localized cortisone injections for temporary relief. However, cortisone is indicated only when the tendons to be injected aren't under a constant load. Cortisone tends to "dry out" the tissue, causing *necrosis* (tissue damage). This can lead to a ruptured tendon.

- In persistent cases, a relatively simple surgical procedure can save the day. The surgeon removes a small section of the offending IT band, eliminating the pain.

Plica Syndrome

DESCRIPTION

A *plica* is a piece of *synovial tissue* (lining of the joint) that becomes inflamed.

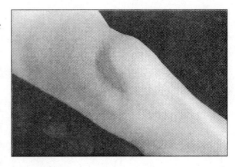

Only 70 percent of humans have this anatomical structure because it's an embryological remnant. Pain occurs when the plica is trapped between the *patella* (kneecap) and the *femur* (thighbone).

SYMPTOMS

- Sharp pain on the medial (inner side) of the knee in the crease beside the patella. In rare cases, the pain is felt in other parts of the knee.

- It begins as an ache. Most medical professionals initially mistake it for chondromalacia. It feels like something is being sawed against the sharp, bony edges of the patella and femur.

CAUSES

- Plica syndrome often accompanies a saddle that's set too low.

- Overuse is often a factor.

- Knock-knees and flat feet load the connective tissue on the inside of the knee, pulling the plica tight like a string.

TREATMENT

- Rest off the bike.

- Ice as many as three times a day for 15-20 minutes each time.

- Take a non-steroidal anti-inflammatory drug (NSAID).

- Change activities, perhaps substituting fast walking for cycling.

IF THESE REMEDIES DON'T WORK

- Because the plica is often irritated by a saddle that's too low, raising the saddle about 3 mm can often reduce the symptoms.

- Persistent plica pain of a year or more can be stopped by surgical removal of the offending tissue.

Inflammation of the Medial Patellar Femoral Ligament

DESCRIPTION

The *medial patellar femoral ligament* is a band of tissue running from the inner border of the kneecap to the thighbone.

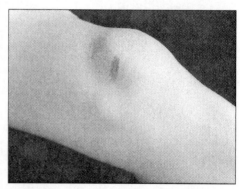

Only about 70 percent of the population has an identifiable MPFL. It rarely becomes inflamed except in repetitive sports such as cycling.

SYMPTOMS

- A sharp pain on the medial (inner side) of the knee. It can be isolated to a pinpoint pain on the inner edge of the kneecap.

CAUSES

- A low saddle.

- Pedals with too much float.
- Knock knees, flat feet or tight ilio-tibial bands.

TREATMENT

- Ice applied directly to the spot of pain, as many as three times a day for 15-20 minutes.
- Rest off the bike.
- Sometimes a cortisone injection helps.
- Orthotics, forefoot varus wedging and a professional bike fit often help knock-kneed or flat-footed riders.
- Avoid pedals that allow excessive float. They make the problem worse because the MPFL has to work hard to control the kneecap if there's too much tibial rotation caused by too much float.

IF THESE REMEDIES DON'T WORK

- In advanced and persistent cases, steroid injections can be used after six months of trying the less-aggressive treatments listed above.
- If steroid injections don't produce improvement in an additional six months, this condition can be treated with a surgical release of the ligament.

Pes Anserine Bursitis/Tendinitis

DESCRIPTION

Pes anserine is Latin for "goosefoot," a description of what the three *medial* (inner side of the knee) hamstrings look like in a dissected cadaver where they connect to the tibia. Aren't you glad you asked?

SYMPTOMS

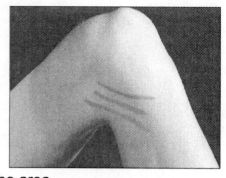

- Sharp pain on medial side of the knee, about one inch below its center.

- Swelling, with tenderness and pain when you touch or stretch the area.

CAUSES

- An excessively high saddle.

- Riding a fixed-gear (track) bike.

- A pedal system with too much float.

- Knock knees and/or flat feet.

- A too-wide stance on the pedals.

TREATMENT

- This condition is often caused by a saddle that's too high so lowering the saddle about 3 mm can provide relief.

- Apply ice as many as three times a day for 15-20 minutes each time.

- Take a non-steroidal anti-inflammatory drug (NSAID) with food.

IF THESE REMEDIES DON'T WORK

- Get fitted for a good cycling orthotic.

- Switch to pedals with less float (less than 8 degrees of rotation to each side of neutral). Pedals that allow generous foot rotation make the problem worse because the pes anserine has to work hard to stabilize the resulting *tibial* (lower leg) rotation.

Biceps Femoris Tendinitis or Popliteus Tendinitis

DESCRIPTION

Biceps femoris is the hamstring that attaches to the outer side of the knee on the back of the *fibula* (lower leg). Tendinitis here is often confused with IT band syndrome, but the pain 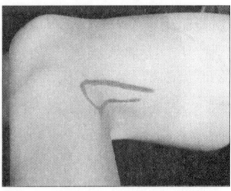 is lower down the outside of the knee.

Pain in the same area may also involve the *popliteus*, a muscle smaller than your little finger. It attaches in the same general area as the biceps femoris and controls the rotation of the tibia. Both conditions are treated the same way.

SYMPTOMS

- Pain on the outer side of the knee about one inch below the middle of the joint and slightly above the bony protuberance.

CAUSES

- A too-high saddle or riding a fixed-gear bike.

- Bow-legged people often suffer this problem.

- Pedals with excessive float make the problem worse because the biceps femoris and popliteal tendons have to work hard to stabilize the resulting excessive tibial rotation.

TREATMENT

- Apply ice as many as three times a day for 15-20 minutes each time.

- Take a non-steroidal anti-inflammatory drug (NSAID) with food.

- Lower the saddle about 3 mm.

- Switch to a pedal system with limited or no float.

IF THESE REMEDIES DON'T WORK

- Because biceps femoris tendinitis is often caused by riding a fixed-gear (track) bike, changing to a bike with a freewheel often alleviates the problem. While riding a fixed gear, the hamstrings are used to decelerate, putting them under load and sometimes irritating the biceps femoris tendon.

Answers to FAQ: Knees

Q: How should I care for knees on rides?

- **Keep your knees warm**. Riding in chilly temperatures with bare knees is a recipe for trouble. The knee's tendons lie exposed near the skin's surface. My rule is to cover your knees with leg warmers or tights if the air temperature is below 65 degrees.

- **Warm up.** Your knees need at least 15 minutes of gradual spinning to get the blood flowing. Start in a small gear and gradually build up both the resistance and the cadence until you're sweating lightly and your knees feel loose. Blasting out of your driveway in the big ring and attacking the first hill can lead to disaster.

- **Spin**. Keep your cadence between 80 and 110 rpm on the flats and no lower than 70 rpm when you're climbing in the saddle. If you're standing while climbing you can go a bit lower, but not much. Low cadences and big gears are an unholy alliance, putting major strain on knee tendons. Look at the pros—they spin at high cadences with a pedal stroke that's silky smooth.

- **Build mileage gradually**. The standard recommendation is to increase mileage no more than 10 percent from one week to the next. You need to let your knees adapt to the workload.

- **Change with caution**. You knees are creatures of habit. They don't like new strains or stresses. So, if you've been riding on flat roads all season, work into climbing gradually. If you decide to install longer crankarms, don't ride 100 miles the first time out on the new equipment. Go easy.

Q: What if I have a pre-existing knee injury?

Sometimes, a person's bike fits fine and he undertakes a smart, gradual and moderate training program. But a knee hurts anyway. In this case, suspect a pre-existing injury that has flared up from cycling.

One example is a slight cartilage tear suffered in another sport, such as football. Cycling is great for this sort of chronic knee problem, so reduce mileage and continue to ride. Your body should soon adapt. But if it doesn't, see an orthopedist or physical therapist.

Q: What are custom cycling orthotics, and do I need them?

Orthotics are used inside shoes. They are a great way to correct the biomechanics of your feet. They are made for your unique feet, so offer support far superior to generic insoles or footbeds.

Most orthotics are meant for walking or running. Therefore, they are "heel posted," meaning that they are designed for a stride where the heel hits first. They are also relatively short, extending from heel to just behind the ball of the foot.

But in cycling, it's not the heel but the ball of the foot that makes contact with the pedal. As a result, cycling orthotics are "forefoot posted." They extend beyond the arch nearly to the toes.

Do you need custom orthotics for cycling? Consider using orthotics if you pronate badly (ankles tilt inward), have flat feet or have persistent knee pain that proper bike fit and other healthy-knee measures in this book don't cure.

Be sure your orthotics are made by a cycling-knowledgeable podiatrist, physical therapist or athletic trainer.

Q: How can I keep my knees healthy off the bike?

- **Don't squat or kneel excessively**. Squatting loads the back of the kneecap, while kneeling pushes the kneecap into the bony groove of the femur (thighbone). This can cause damage.

- **Don't climb or descend hills or stairs**. Walking down exposes any weaknesses you have in muscle groups such as your quadriceps' vastus medialis. Running downhill is especially hard on knees. Mountain runners are used to the pounding of hard descents on rubbly trails, but they've trained long and hard to accustom their knees to the abuse.

- **Don't do weight exercises that isolate the kneecap.** These include full-range leg extensions and full squats. These exercises cause compressing and shearing forces on the back of the kneecap. When doing leg extensions, limit movement to the final 25 degrees before your knees straighten. On squats and leg presses, don't bend knees more than 90 degrees.

If you do everything right and your knees still hurt, seek an expert's help.

Chapter 6
Back and Neck

Low-back pain is the No. 2 complaint of cyclists (knee pain is No. 1) and the frequency is rising as the population ages.

Among the general population, low-back pain afflicts 80 percent of the adult population. About 10 million people miss work each day because of it. It doesn't seem to matter if you are a sedentary desk jockey or a manual laborer—there's no difference in the incidence of back pain.

Fortunately, about 40 percent of sufferers get better in one week, and almost 90 percent get better in a month, even without specific treatment. But 90 percent of people who experience low-back pain one time are doomed to have recurring episodes. What's worse, with each episode, recovery time lengthens.

There are many causes of low-back pain in the general population, ranging from weak core muscles to nerve damage to aging disks. But for cyclists the causes are fairly simple and they usually boil down to improper bike fit or poor riding position. If you have an existing low-back problem, poor bike fit can make it even worse.

Neck pain is less prevalent in cyclists. But it can be a real plague, especially among long-distance cyclists who hold their head in the riding position for hours at a time. Time trialists and triathletes are likely sufferers, too, because they try to get so low on the bike that they have to crane their neck to see ahead. This loads the joints of the cervical spine.

Back Pain

SYMPTOMS

- Sharp pain in the muscles along the spine, or a dull ache in the area just above the pelvis. Biomechanical low-back pain might result from degenerative disk disease, *lordosis* (swayback), *scoliosis* (lateral curvature of the spine) or age-related wear and tear.

- Sharp pain between the shoulder blades. Upper-back pain has a list of diagnoses similar to low-back pain. Included are degenerative disk disease, *kyphosis* (humpback), scoliosis, age-related wear and tear, muscle weakness and muscle spasms due to poor bike fit.

CAUSES

- According to laboratory studies, the most common cause of back pain in cyclists is a leg length inequality, either real or functional.

- Incorrect bike fit is a frequent contributor, especially too much reach to the handlebar leading to muscle fatigue and spasms.

- Lack of "core" strength in the torso can cause fatigue and back pain.

- Back pain may plague cyclists who attempt mileage significantly greater than they are used to doing.

TREATMENT

- If you have a conventional stem, pull it farther out of the steerer tube to raise the handlebar. A higher riding position will reduce strain on the low back by lessening forward bending.

CAUTION! When raising the handlebar, never exceed the maximum height line that's etched into the stem. If you do, the stem could break off during a ride. You will need more than this book to remedy what happens after that.

- You can also get a higher position by loosening the stem's binder bolt to rotate the handlebar upward slightly, raising the brake levers.

- On bikes with threadless headsets and stems, adjustment usually requires buying a new stem with more *rise* (upward angle). Check first to see if your stem is reversible, providing more rise if it's turned over.

- If your reach to the handlebar is excessive, a higher stem may alleviate the problem even if it's the same length. A bike's head tube is slanted to the rear, so raising the stem also shortens the reach.

- Get a professional bike fit by a qualified coach, trainer or shop employee. Remember that there's a big difference between a coach's "performance-based" fit compared to a bike shop's "comfort-based" fit. Be sure you know what you need for meeting your goals in the sport.

- If stem and position adjustments don't work, you may need a bike with a shorter top tube. Get the advice of a qualified professional (or two) before making this major investment.

- Practice good riding habits. Move around on the bike to take pressure off your back. Change hand positions and stand up for one minute in every five, even if the terrain doesn't encourage it. On long seated climbs, slide to the back of the saddle, to the middle and then to the front.

- Ice and anti-inflammatory medication often helps.

- A commercial bandage impregnated with a counter-irritant ("hot stuff") often provides some relief, probably because you feel the heat of the wintergreen rather than the back pain.

IF THESE REMEDIES DON'T WORK

Check to rule out a leg-length inequality (LLI). This can be done two ways:

1. The simplest method is a *standing AP pelvis*, an x-ray of your hip region done from the front while you're standing. The technician can measure the difference in the height of your femoral heads to determine your functional leg length inequality. This doesn't, however, tell in which leg segments an inequality exists. The technician will have to judge this. It's an inaccurate science that takes considerable expertise.

2. LLI also can be determined from a *scanogram* x-ray, although this can be difficult for an inexperienced technician. Your leg bones are actually measured by including a meter stick in the x-ray image. I rarely do scanogram x-rays anymore. Using the standing AP pelvis and a good clinical exam, I can usually find the LLI location.

LLI's of as little as 3 mm can be symptomatic in some riders, especially those doing high mileage or who have a history of low-back pain. The solution is to shim the cleat or shift the foot in relation to the pedal (as described below).

Strengthen your abs and low-back musculature with crunches and partial back extensions, and increase low back flexibility with appropriate stretches. A physical therapist can teach you several effective ones.

TIP **See a qualified physical therapist to get an exercise and stretching regimen designed for you. You'll need the correct diagnosis of your problem to get the best results.**

Answers to FAQ: Cleat Shimming

Q: When should I shim a cleat?

If you have a leg-length inequality (LLI) of 3 mm or greater accompanied by back pain, it's important to heed the following advice.

For walking or running, most orthopedists won't adjust for a LLI until the difference between legs is 6 mm or more.

In cycling, if the LLI is less than 6 mm, I don't use a shim. Instead, I move the cleat on the short-leg side forward on the shoe sole 1-2 mm. You can move the cleat on the long-leg foot backward to get the same affect. Rarely do you have to compensate for the full amount of the LLI.

These techniques have the effect of making the short-leg foot slightly longer to compensate for the leg length difference. If the LLI is over 6 mm, it requires a shim.

Q: How do I shim my cleat?

The shim goes between the shoe sole and the cleat (photo). It's green in this example. Look and Look-compatible road cleats are the easiest to shim, while Shimano SPD cleats (both road and off-road) are slightly harder. Other brands vary from fairly easy to difficult. Several makes of high-end road cleats are im-

possible to shim.

Shoe repair shops and companies specializing in prosthetic devices can shim your cleats if you explain what you want. Or, you can do it yourself.

Here's how:

The thickness of the under-cleat shim should be half of the short leg's inequality.

1. Choose a material to use as a shim. Neolite, available in shoe repair shops, works well for Look road cleats. Fairly hard plastic or aluminum bar stock is often used for Shimano SPD cleats. The material should be hard enough to resist compression but soft enough for the serrated bottom of the cleat to make an impression. You don't want the cleat to slide when the bolts are tightened or when it's entering or exiting the pedal.

2. The shim should generally be half the amount of your leg-length inequality. Why? Because your body has already adjusted for much of the LLI via various physical compensations. Adjusting for the entire amount would be overkill. So, if your LLI is 8 mm, the shim should be 3-4 mm thick.

3. Obtain longer bolts to accommodate the added thickness of the shim. Take one of the stock bolts to a hardware store.

4. Cut the shim material in the shape of the cleat.

5. Drill bolt holes.

6. Glue the shim to the shoe sole after you align the bolt holes. Hold it with a C-clamp till completely dry.

If you have the 3-hole Campagnolo cleat, the shim can't protrude outside the cleat or it won't engage properly.

7. Re-attach the cleat.

8. On shoes with recessed cleat pockets, the shimmed cleat will protrude above the sole, causing it to touch the ground when you walk. If this annoys you, build up the sole around the cleat with Shoe Goo, a product for repairing running shoe soles. It's available in shoe repair shops or sporting goods stores.

Q: My scanogram x-ray showed a leg-length discrepancy of 8 mm. Most of it is in my femur rather than in my lower leg. Does this change how I shim my cleat?

A femoral LLI is hard to correct. When one thighbone is shorter than the other you can't sit square on the saddle. The center of the knee wants to be directly over the pedal axle, and that's impossible when the upper legs are of different lengths. Riders with this problem can't get completely comfortable on the bike no matter what they do.

The solution is to shim and move the short-leg cleat. For example, with an 8-mm LLI where most of the difference is femoral, I'd shim the cleat 3 mm and move the short-leg cleat forward on the shoe sole about 2 mm. (Remember that we don't compensate for the full amount so this doesn't add up to 8 mm.) Sliding the cleat forward has the effect of lengthening the foot and leg, helping center that knee over the pedal.

'Shermer Neck'

DESCRIPTION

Shermer neck is named after Michael Shermer, a Race Across America competitor who suffered from what can be termed neck failure. Things got so bad that his crew members constructed a makeshift brace from bungee cords to hold up his head as he rode. Shermer isn't the only RAAM rider to suffer debilitating neck fatigue and pain, but he was the first and, now, most famous.

SYMPTOMS

- Your neck feels tight and painful after you've been riding a while.

- It's hard to turn your head to the side or look behind for traffic.

- In extreme cases, such as riding 350 miles day after day in the Race Across America, the neck muscles go into spasm. Like Shermer, riders can no longer hold up their head.

CAUSES

- Improper bike fit, primarily excessive reach to the handlebar that makes you crane your neck to see ahead

- Insufficient strength in the neck muscles.

- Riding long distances without sufficient breaks.

- Riding in an aero position that requires you to hyperextend your neck to see down the road.

- Locking your head in a straight-forward position for minutes on end.

TREATMENT

- Raise your stem or install a shorter, high-rise stem.

- If you're on aero bars, raise them so you can see ahead without strain.

- Change position frequently as you ride. Stand often so your neck is supported by your spine rather than your muscles. Frequently turn your head from side to side and up and down to stretch and relax your neck.

- Tilt your head slightly to the left or right of vertical, rather than lock into the dead center position.

IF THESE REMEDIES DON'T WORK

- Strengthen your neck with exercises provided by a physical therapist or cycling coach.

- Gradually increase mileage so your neck becomes conditioned to holding your head in the riding position for longer periods.

Chapter 7
Foot and Ankle

It's generally agreed that foot pain can be the most agonizing in our sport. Greg LeMond, three-time Tour de France winner, was a famous sufferer and needed custom shoes to alleviate his misery. But with modern anatomical shoes as well as custom cycling orthotics, there's no reason you have to suffer the agony of de feet.

In an attempt to develop better cycling shoes, I teamed with Specialized Bicycle Components, Inc., in 2000 to design the Body Geometry shoe line. The technical features include a longitudinal arch support, forefoot varus wedge as part of the outsole, and an arch cushion and a metatarsal arch support as part of the sock liner. Body Geometry shoes should reduce the need for custom orthotics in up to 90 percent of cyclists.

Hot Foot

DESCRIPTION

Cyclists use the general term *hot foot* to describe a number of foot discomforts that produce the sensation of heat as well as pain.

SYMPTOMS

- Numb toes.
- Pain under the ball of the foot.

- The sensation that someone is searing the bottom of your foot with a blowtorch.

CAUSES

- The unpleasant symptoms (called *metatarsalgia*) are generally caused by nerves squeezed between the *metatarsal heads* (foot bones) in the ball of the foot just behind the toes. A *Morton's neuroma*, in contrast, is a specific inflamed nerve between the third and fourth metatarsal spaces.

- Tight shoes are often the culprit. Leather cycling shoes, common 15 years ago, stretched with use to give feet room. But today's synthetic uppers don't stretch much. If shoes are tight when you buy them, they will remain tight and are likely to cause problems, especially on long rides.

- Most cycling shoes are simply a flat-bottom box for your feet. But most feet aren't flat on the bottom. Cyclists need anatomical footbeds or orthotics to support their feet in these badly designed shoes.

- Unsupported forefoot *varus* often causes hot foot.

- A small pedal concentrates pressure on one part of the foot instead of spreading pressure like a large-platform pedal.

  This generally isn't a problem with high-quality road shoes because their rigid sole distributes the pressure. But shoes with flexible soles—including most mountain bike shoes suitable for walking—usually compress where the pedal contacts the sole, passing the pressure to the foot.

- Feet can be bruised on the sole by hard pedaling or lengthy climbs.

- Some narrow, bony, thin feet are extremely susceptible to hot foot because they lack padding. Fat, meaty, wide feet are at high risk, too, because they're often jammed into cycling shoes that are too narrow.

TREATMENT

- To redistribute pressure on your feet, move your cleats rearward about 2 mm and lower your saddle the same amount. You should feel significant improvement.

- Insoles or orthotics with a *metatarsal bump* usually help. A metatarsal bump is a small domed area in the footbed slightly behind the ball of the foot (photo). This spreads the bones of the forefoot, taking pressure off the nerves between them.

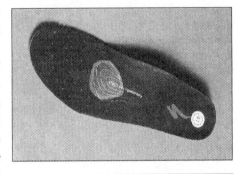

A metatarsal bump spreads the forefoot to reduce the risk of painful nerve compression.

- Some riders have good luck with so-called *metatarsal arch buttons*. You stick these small foam buttons to the insole just behind the ball of the foot. They work like the metatarsal bump in orthotics. Find these buttons in the foot care section of a drugstore, or make your own from dense foam.

- To make more room in tight shoes, install thinner insoles or use thinner cycling socks. This can be a quick fix if you're on a tour and developing pain.

IF THESE REMEDIES DON'T WORK

- Switch to pedals with a larger platform for better support.

- Wear shoes with a wider toe box, a stiffer sole and an anatomical footbed. Specialized Body Geometry shoes are the best example.

- Plastic wedges, such as Bicycle Fitting System's Bio-Wedges, can be put between the cleat and the sole to level the foot on the pedal and distribute pressure.

- In advanced cases of Morton's neuroma, should several cortisone injections fail, surgery is indicated.

- Long-distance cyclists, especially those competing in grueling events like the Furnace Creek 508, Paris-Brest-Paris or the Race Across America, often want their cleats so far behind the ball of the foot that they drill new holes in the sole. I don't recommend extreme measures like this unless hot foot persists after you've tried the above remedies.

Achilles Tendinitis

DESCRIPTION

An inflammation of the *Achilles tendon* on the back of the ankle, between where the tendon attaches to the heel bone and where it merges with the calf muscle.

SYMPTOMS

- Pain in the tendon.

- There may be an area of swelling like a small grape on the tendon.

- In some cases, the tendon squeaks like a rusty hinge when you move the foot up and down by bending the ankle.

CAUSES

- Overuse. Increasing mileage too quickly or lots of climbing when you aren't accustomed to it.

- Faulty foot mechanics such as excessive *pronation* (inward tilting of the ankle).

- A tight Achilles tendon.

- Having the cleat positioned too far forward so you are pedaling "on your toes." This causes excessive use of the calf muscle during the pedal stroke.

TREATMENT

- Rest off the bike.

- Apply ice up to three times per day for 10-15 minutes each time.

- Take a non-steroidal anti-inflammatory drug (NSAID) with food.

- To reduce strain on the Achilles, move your foot forward on the pedal by moving the cleat toward the heel of the shoe. Then lower the saddle an amount equal to the distance you moved the cleats. Stay symmetrical by moving both cleats and treating both ankles equally, even though only one may be giving you a problem.

- If you must keep riding on a tour, tape the ankle to lessen movement and reduce stress on the tendon.

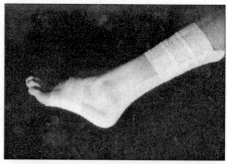

TIP **To tape your ankle for Achilles tendon relief, point your toe down about 30 degrees and run a pre-stretched strip of 3-inch elastic tape from the ball of the foot to the heel, then up the Achilles to the middle of the calf. Hold the bandage in place with tape applied like you'd normally tape an ankle for stability. The idea is to immobilize the ankle so much that you can't *dorsiflex* it (bring your toes toward your shin) while you pedal. This lessens strain on the Achilles.**

- To stretch a tight Achilles tendon, stand 2-3 feet from a wall or tree. Extend your arms and lean in by bending your elbows while keeping your heels on the ground. This is a good pre-ride stretch if you tend to be tight. Check with a physical therapist for other stretching exercises.

IF THESE REMEDIES DON'T WORK

- Custom cycling orthotics often help by correcting rear-foot angulation.

- In some cases, an excessive amount of pedal float irritates the Achilles tendon because it has to work hard to stabilize the foot on the pedal. Switching to pedals with limited float may offer relief.

A Word about Ankling

Some riders believe that they should pedal with a pronounced ankling motion. In other words, with their toes pointing down at the bottom of the stroke to help pull the pedal around with the strength of their calf.

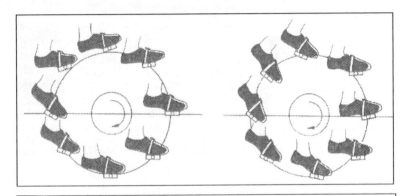

Ankling is a concept as old as toe straps and platform pedals. A relatively natural pedal stoke is shown at left. The illustration at right shows an attempt to "ankle" and bring the calf muscle into play. *(Adapted from "Science of Cycling")*

This once-popular technique is now outmoded. We know from EMG studies where we measure the electrical activity of muscles that calves are poor power producers in cycling. Most of the power in the pedal stroke is generated by the quadriceps of the thigh and the glutes of the butt. Calves are merely the cables to transfer the power of the quads to your foot and pedal.

Some people naturally ankle modestly, but when we do 3-D studies of pedal strokes there's typically 10 degrees or less of total ankle flexion. It's incredibly small.

I think ankling is an adjustment for the location of the tibial shaft in the pedal stroke. As your foot comes over the top, you dorsiflex (drop your heel slightly). As you approach the bottom of the stroke, you point your toe down slightly. But an excessive ankling motion is probably a waste of energy.

My advice is not to consciously think about ankling. Instead, try to apply pressure to the pedal all the way around the stroke. Greg LeMond's advice is still on target—pull your foot through the bottom of the pedal stroke by imagining that you're scraping mud off your shoe. The next thing you know, your foot will be back at the top.

LeMond, incidentally, was often pictured with his heel lower than his toes as his foot passed through the bottom of the pedal stroke—especially on climbs.

Studies done on Olympic cyclists show that even the best riders don't produce power on the upstroke. The pedal goes around so fast that they can't actually pull the foot up as the pedal rises. The exceptions are mountain bikers who are nearly stalled on technical terrain and amputee riders who pedal with only one leg.

Chapter 8
Hands, Arms, Shoulders

Among the three areas of contact between the body and the bike (crotch, hands and feet), the crotch gets much of the attention. After all, a case of saddle sores is an ailment you won't soon forget.

But hand problems might be more debilitating because we need our hands for our jobs and other daily activities. For a surgeon, a musician, a woodworker or a writer, numb fingers can be career-threatening. Fortunately, tingly digits can be avoided with proper bike fit and judicious padding in gloves and handlebars.

Arms and shoulder injuries in cyclists are almost always from contact of another nature—with the ground. Usually, these crash-induced injuries are straightforward orthopedic cases and they heal quickly.

Cyclist's Palsy, Carpal Tunnel Syndrome

DESCRIPTION

Pain and numbness in fingers.

SYMPTOM

- Your hands and fingers tingle and become numb.

CAUSES

- *Cyclist's palsy* is caused by nerve compression in the hand against the handlebar or brake lever hoods. If you ride with your wrist cocked and angled towards the thumb, you're at risk for numbness in the ring and small fingers. This problem often affects mountain bikers because flat bars encourage a bent wrist and don't allow many changes in hand position.

- If you ride on the brake hoods of a road bike with the wrist cocked and angled toward the little finger, you're at risk for *carpal tunnel syndrome* with numbness afflicting the thumb and index finger.

TREATMENT

- Don't bend your wrists when you grip the handlebar because it leads to nerve entrapment and hand pain.

- Use a flat bar that angles to the rear so your wrist isn't bent as much.

- On a road bike, vary your hand position every few minutes from the drops to the brake hoods to the top near the stem.

- Stand frequently to alter the pressure on your hands.

- Numb and tingly hands often improve with gel-padded cycling gloves, cushy grips on a flat bar or padded tape on a drop bar.

- Another culprit is a saddle that is tilted down. This causes you to slide toward the handlebar, putting your weight forward and onto your hands. Make sure your saddle is level with the ground.

IF THESE REMEDIES DON'T WORK

- Get the weight off your hands by moving your handlebar higher and closer to the saddle. The easiest ways to do this are with a shorter stem that has more rise, or (for traditional quill stems) installing a model that has a long shank.

- If you use a flat bar, consider a "riser" or down-hill model. This style makes you sit up a bit more, relieving pressure on your hands.

A Word about Cycling Gloves

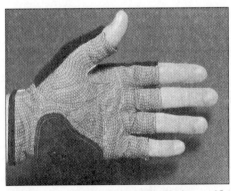

Always wear gloves, even for short errand rides. Properly pad-ded, anatomic gloves are neces-sary for comfort. They protect your hands and associ-ated nerves from road vibration and pressure from the handlebar. If you ride off-road, con-sider long-finger gloves for added protection.

Gloves are most valuable if you crash. Some of the worst abrasions occur on the palm of the hands because most people automatically try to break a fall by reaching out.

When palms slide across the pavement, the result-ing deep cuts and abrasions are one of the most painful injuries you can imagine. They heal slowly, too, because you're always using your hands.

Navicular Wrist Fracture

DESCRIPTION

The fracture of a small bone on the thumb side of the wrist. It's called a *snuffbox fracture* because if you angle your thumb up, you can see an indentation at the end of your wrist between two tendons (photo). This is where people used to put snuff so they

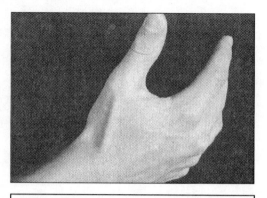

The indentation below the thumb marks the location of this injury (as well as a handy place to lay snuff).

could inhale it. The pain of a *navicular fracture* occurs in the same place.

SYMPTOM

- Your wrist hurts on the inner base of the forearm where the wrist and thumb join.

CAUSE

- Extending your hand to catch yourself in a fall.

TREATMENT

- This is an especially difficult fracture to diagnose. Often there's no deformity, but it stays sore for days just above the base of the thumb and there's little or no improvement. Even if you think it's only a slow-healing bruise, go for an x-ray. It may take several x-rays over time to identify the fracture. It may not show up until it starts to heal.

- To avoid surgery, this injury should be immobilized for several months until healing is complete. Even so, many riders have raced successfully in a navicular cast.

Broken Collarbone, Shoulder Separation

DESCRIPTION

A *fractured clavicle* (collarbone) is one of the most common injuries in cycling. A *shoulder separation* occurs when the joint between the shoulder blade and collarbone is wrenched apart by impact. This *acromioclavicular (A-C) joint* (photo) is the bump on the top of your shoulder, about 2 inches inboard.

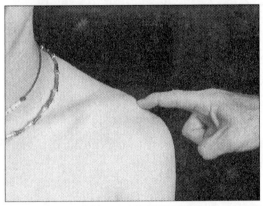

Here's the location of the A-C joint.

SYMPTOMS

- In the case of collarbone fractures, you'll feel pain and see swelling and perhaps discoloration of the collarbone area.

- Sometimes you'll recall hearing a popping sound as you hit the ground.

- Often you can feel and see a bump on the collarbone that wasn't there before.

- If you separated your A-C joint, the pain and swelling may be farther out on the shoulder where the collarbone meets the shoulder blade.

- A shoulder separation may result in a "step shoulder," a prominent dip of the outer inch or two when viewed from the front. Compare it to the other shoulder in a mirror.

CAUSE

- Broken collarbones and shoulder separations result from a fall on your shoulder and/or outstretched hand.

TREATMENT

- There is no quick fix for these injuries. Riding with either is dangerous because the pain and disability compromise bike handling. Mountain bikers have ridden many miles of rough trails to get to medical help, and pro roadies have continued riding to finish races. But such heroics aren't recommended because they can make things worse and ultimately delay healing.

- See a physician immediately. Go to an emergency room or directly to an orthopedic surgeon.

- For most collarbone fractures, you'll be put in a stabilizing sling or other device for a few weeks until you're comfortable. The broken ends of the bone will find each other and knit back together. (In rare cases, the ends must be pinned together.) Healing usually takes six weeks, but it's okay to ride indoors when you can do it comfortably.

- Most shoulder separations don't require surgery unless they become functional or cosmetic problems over time. The exception is a combination fractured collarbone and AC separation. When these injuries occur together, surgery is usually required.

Chapter 9
Crotch and Skin

Until quite recently, riders sat on hard, plastic-shell saddles that weren't shaped for their anatomy. Shorts were made of wool and had a liner made of leather. This *chamois* was soft when new, but after a few washings it lost its natural oil and assumed the texture of a taco chip.

But now, with modern saddle and cycling short technology, you should be able to find designs that enhance your health and comfort. It may require some trial and error, though.

Crotchitis/Saddle Soreness

DESCRIPTION

These are general terms for soreness in the *perineum* (crotch), where soft tissue meets the saddle. Problems can be as simple as boils or as complicated as *pudendal nerve palsy* (genital numbness), *impotence* (erectile dysfunction), *prostatitis* (inflammation of the prostate gland), or *urethritis* (urinary tract difficulties).

The crotch isn't designed to bear weight, but time in the saddle allows it to adapt. This includes the soft tissue over the *ischial tuberosities* (sit bones), the two points of the pelvis that should contact the saddle.

SYMPTOMS

Skin in the crotch can become red and abraded. Sometimes it erupts in small boils or a painful rash.

89

- Saddle pressure can cause pudendal nerve palsy in both sexes. A male can suffer from saddle-induced prostatitis or impotence, although occurrences are rare.

- Women can experience abraded soft tissue.

- *Ischial bursitis*, marked by pain and swelling directly on the sit bones, can be caused by a hard saddle, a poor-quality chamois or too many miles without sufficient buildup.

- *Urethritis*, marked by a feeling of bladder pressure sometimes with the desire to urinate frequently, occurs with irritation and inflammation of the *urethra* (the tube for the discharge of urine).

CAUSES

- Poor riding position, especially a saddle set too high. This makes you rock your hips as your legs reach the bottom of the stroke, sawing your delicate tissue across the saddle.

- An upward tilted saddle that causes the nose to press into your crotch, or a downward tilt that causes you to slide forward and push yourself back.

- Poor saddle choice. No specific saddle design is right for every rider. The saddle that is crotch nirvana for one rider is pubic purgatory for another. You need to try various designs to find the one that works best for you.

- Failure to wear cycling shorts with a well-constructed liner to pad the crotch and reduce abrasion. The biggest mistake new riders make is wearing underwear with their cycling shorts, or not using cycling shorts at all.

- Poor riding habits, such as not standing enough to relieve pressure and not shifting to various locations on the saddle.

- Riding in rainy or humid weather often causes chafing as wet shorts rub your damp skin.

- Remaining in your cycling shorts after a ride can lead to boils because the bacteria have time to penetrate and infect abraded skin.

TREATMENT

- Always ride in high-quality cycling shorts that have a soft, absorbent, padded liner (photo). Some companies have liners designed to reduce pressure on the nerves and blood vessels in the perineum.

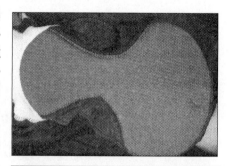

Many shorts liners come treated with an antibacterial agent to reduce the risk of skin infection.

- Try a skin lubricant to minimize abrasion. Some lubes are water-soluble, others are petroleum-based. The former absorb well and wash easily from your skin and shorts. The latter have more staying power, especially in wet conditions. I recommend petroleum-based products that contain antibiotics.

- If you have to ride a good distance in the rain— on a tour, for example—a coating of petroleum jelly reduces the risk of chafing.

- As soon as possible after every ride, get out of your cycling shorts and into the shower. Don't hang around and let your shorts become a Petri dish. After cleaning up, put on loose-fitting garments so your skin will stay dry.

- Wash your cycling shorts after *every* use.

- If you have saddle problems on a tour when you must ride every day, slide the saddle forward 5-10 mm to move pressure to a new area. This change won't significantly alter your correct position on the bike because your sit bones will automatically slide back to the wider part of the saddle.

- Your weight should be on your sit bones, not on the soft tissue in front of them. Be sure your handlebar isn't too low or too far from the saddle. An excessive reach makes you roll forward and sit on your soft tissue. If you're swaybacked, the problem can be worse.

- For ischial bursitis, use ice, NSAIDs and rest off the bike. A cortisone injection can provide quick relief. To keep it from recurring, wear two pairs of shorts for more padding. You may want to cut a round hole in the liner of the inner pair, directly over the painful area.

- A topical prescription medication such as erythromycin can be effective for spot treatment of sores. Bag Balm can be used to soothe chafing. This nonprescription product, developed to heal the irritated teats of cows, is available in drug stores.

- A large, deep or stubborn boil may require treatment with antibiotics. See your doctor for an evaluation and prescription.

IF THESE REMEDIES DON'T WORK

- Most saddle problems can be fixed with good bike fit, so visit a competent shop, a licensed cycling coach or knowledgeable athletic trainer. Remember, there's a big difference between fits for performance and for comfort. Be sure to explain your cycling goals.

- Tight hamstrings stop you from rolling your pelvis forward to sit properly on the saddle. On the other hand, a tight low back makes you roll too far forward, putting weight on your perineum. Consult a physical therapist for appropriate stretching exercises.

- Check for a leg-length inequality.

- Choose a new saddle with a different shape and amount of padding.

A Word about Saddles and Shorts

Maybe I was wrong when I said that reach to the handlebar is the most personal part of cycling. It may actually be the choice of a saddle and shorts!

Remember that the same saddle won't work well for everyone. Just as there is significant variation in face shapes among the general population, there's a wide difference in crotch shapes as well.

Roger Minkow, M.D., the designer of the Specialized Body Geometry saddles—the most popular saddle line in the world—admits that one model won't work for all riders.

Here's the key point: There are saddle and shorts designs out there that are right for you. You just have to keep looking.

A good shop should be willing to switch the saddle on a bike it sold you if you can't get comfortable after a few weeks. Of course, this can't happen with shorts for sanitary reasons.

Once you find a liner design that works for you, buy several pairs of those shorts. If your favorite model is discontinued, look for the same general shape and stitching pattern when you need more shorts.

Saddles are expensive, but this mustn't stop you from finding a model that fits your unique anatomy. To minimize the expense of trial and error, ask a shop if it has loaner saddles you can try. Or, organize an informal saddle-swapping club. Find several cyclists who are willing to trade saddles or even buy new ones to pass around for others to ride.

When you finally find a saddle that works or you, buy one for each of your bikes!

Road Rash

DESCRIPTION

Skin abrasions on the thigh, calf, buttocks, forearm, elbows, back or shoulder from sliding along the pavement or trail.

SYMPTOMS

- Red, oozing, raw scrapes.

- Although road rash is usually superficial, there can be deeper cuts imbedded in the abrasions—depending on what you fell on. A gravelly "chip-and-seal" surface is the worst. The result is like a cheese grater on your skin if you fall and slide.

CAUSE

- You fell off!

TREATMENT

- Abrasions must be thoroughly scrubbed clean to avoid infection and prevent "tattooing" of the skin from embedded asphalt oils. It's often best to seek a physician or emergency room. They'll use a topical anesthetic to deaden the pain while they dig out embedded dirt and gravel. They'll also use sterile brushes, thus reducing the chance of infection. If you don't have soap, baby shampoo works well.

- Some cycling events offer wound-care service. Check with medical support before you do the job yourself.

- Road rash heals much faster, and with less scarring, if you keep it moist. Wash the wound gently several times a day, then apply a "wet" dressing that's permeated with antibiotic ointment. The idea is never to let a scab form. You want the wound to heal from the inside out.

- To reduce pain, take acetaminophen (Tylenol) according to label directions during the first 48 hours. After this, you can switch to a NSAID if you prefer.

- Be alert for signs of infection. These include redness in the wound or on its edges, fever, nausea, and perhaps swelling in nearby lymph nodes. If these signs appear, see your doctor.

IF THESE REMEDIES DON'T WORK

- Road rash is often accompanied by underlying bruises. This can lead to a systemic infection when the abrasion "communicates" with the *hematoma* (pool of blood) under the skin. If you experience fever, muscle aches or see red streaks radiating from the abrasion, immediately go to your physician or an emergency room.

- Untreated hematomas may turn to scar tissue or calcify, hardening so they produce pain and limited motion. Hip hematomas in particular often are undertreated and become cosmetically deforming. They need to be compressed and iced. If you develop a "saddlebag" of swelling in the hip area after a fall, see a physician. In the meantime, apply a compression wrap 24 hours a day for at least a week.

- Always get immediate medical help if you're deeply bruised and scraped. You need to rule out injuries that are more serious and have your wounds professionally cleaned.

Answers to FAQ: Skin Problems

Q: How can I prevent road rash or lessen the consequences?

Obviously, good bike-handling skills help you stay upright in tricky situations.

Practice cornering in a dirt field while wearing protective clothing. Riding a mountain or cyclocross bike off-road accustoms you to having the rear wheel slide around. Loss of traction on the road will be less frightening.

Another good drill is to ride side-by-side with a friend on a grassy field. Go slow and practice bumping shoulders and elbows. Then when contact is made in a group on the road, you'll be accustomed to the experience.

Keep pedaling when you feel contact. You'll be able to maintain momentum and ride through many bumps.

Wear a light undershirt beneath your jersey. If you fall, the jersey will slide on the undershirt and absorb some of the friction that would otherwise abrade your skin.

Gloves are always a good idea because they protect your palms, a body part that particularly slow to heal. And of course, always wear a helmet.

Also, consider shaving your legs. Racers and serious recreational cyclists shave for a number of reasons.

- Shaved legs make massage easier because the therapist's hands can rub the skin directly without irritating the hair follicles.

- Hairless legs are easier to clean after a wet and dirty ride.

- Hair creates more friction than smooth skin during a sliding fall, resulting in a worse abrasion.

- Abrasions on shaved legs are easier to scrub clean and bandage.

- Shaved legs look a lot nicer sticking out of tight Lycra cycling shorts!

For the first shave of the season, most riders use hair clippers to harvest the winter's growth. Then they shave off the stubble in the bathtub with a razor and shaving cream. Thereafter, shaving once every seven days or so should be sufficient. Consider using a moisturizing cream to prevent skin dryness.

Q: What belongs in a "crash kit" for events?

I checked with my teammate Drew Geer, M.D., who is an emergency room physician. He recommends enough supplies to clean and dress all the injuries sustained in a crash from the time you hit the pavement to the time of healing. Here is Dr. Geer's list:

BASIC ROAD RASH KIT

Gauze pads	4x4 in.
Non-stick bandage	3x4 in.
Non-stick bandage	3x8 in.
Gauze roll	2 in.
Gauze roll	4 in.
Tape (silk or plastic to hold dressings)	1 in.
Ace bandage (to wrap dressings)	4 in.
Scissors for cutting dressing	
Antibiotic ointment	
Optional	
Gloves (latex or latex-free)	
Chemical cold pack	

ADVANCED KIT

These are hospital or prescription items. Your physician may be able to help you obtain them.

3m Microdon dressing	6 x10 cm
3m Microdon dressing	15x15 cm
3m Microdon dressing	9x25 cm
Surgilast netting	4 yards of size #3
Surgilast netting	4 yards of size #5 or 6
Sur-Clens soap	1 oz. vials
Lidocaine jelly (2%)	
Surgical scrub brush	

Q: Do I need stitches?

Again, I defer to Dr. Geer's experience:

"Whether or not you need stitches can only be answered for each wound," says Drew. "The general rule is that if you are asking the question, you probably need them.

"Placement of sutures depends on many factors like the location of the wound, tension on the skin, width and length of the opening, and the amount of time since injury occurred.

"Remember that any laceration will heal without stitches. We use sutures to promote rapid healing and decrease the risk of infection. Lacerations over joints tend to pull apart and are more likely to require stitches.

"Common cycling injuries needing stitches are lacerations over the elbows, knees or knuckles. These lacerations sometimes penetrate into the joints or bursa [a lubricating sack outside the joint]. Suturing is more important if this happens.

"You can wait up to 12 to 16 hours to get stitched up, but sooner is better. After 16 hours the bacteria counts are too high. Closing bacteria inside the laceration leads to infection. There's one exception: a very large wound that wasn't closed within 16 hours could be closed after three to five days because the bacteria numbers decrease at this time."

Q: My skin takes a beating while riding even if I don't crash. How should I prevent sunburn, slow the skin's aging process and treat the occasional bee sting?

You've heard it before and now you're going to hear it again: Always use sunscreen of at least SPF 30 on exposed skin.

Don't forget to use lip salve that contains sunscreen. Your lips are often exposed the sun, but salve is easily rubbed off while drinking or from licking your lips. The lower lip is at greatest risk because it hangs fully exposed to the sun when you're riding hard and breathing with your mouth open. Worse, a drop of saliva or sweat can form on your lower lip and act like a lens to focus the sun's rays on your flesh.

Premature skin aging can be a serious issue for cyclists who spend so much time in sunlight. Avoid sunburn. Wear long-sleeve jerseys and leg warmers until temperatures rise above 65 degrees. If you get sunburned on a tour and have to ride the next day, wear leg and arm coverings even if it's hot.

A bee can fly into an unzipped jersey and sting you painfully before you can get it out. Zip your jersey if you notice bees in the area. Bees can fly into helmet vents, too. Wearing a bandana or head rag under your helmet can protect you from a nasty sting.

If you are allergic to bee stings, seek medical help immediately. If you aren't, you can at least reduce the pain by applying a sting-relief product sold in drugstores. It comes in little one-use tubes that you can carry in your jersey pocket or seat bag.

Chapter 10
Eyes and Head

I can't think of more important body part than your head and eyes. Blindness is one of the worst conditions imaginable, and if ever seen the aftermath of a severe head injury, you won't forget it. That's why it continues to astound me that so many cyclists ride without helmets or eye protection. Wearing both is a simple but highly effective way to safeguard your most precious possessions.

Eye Problems

Something flies in your eye—usually a bug, dirt or a piece of gravel.

SYMPTOMS

- Your eye burns and waters.

- You'll have an irresistible urge to blink even though bike handling may be compromised.

- It may feel like your eyeball is scratched.

- You may see a foreign body lodged in your eye when you look in a mirror.

CAUSES

- Foreign bodies in the eye are usually the result of not wearing cycling-specific eyewear.

- At certain times of the year, or in certain places like on a road through a farm, the air contains more insects than usual. There's a greater chance of getting one in your eye.

- When it's raining, many riders take off their sunglasses because the lenses are too dark or streaked with water. But gritty water thrown up by other riders' wheels can easily get into unprotected eyes.

TREATMENT

- Always use eyewear to deflect bugs and other airborne debris.

- Sunglasses lessen eyestrain from squinting, and eye fatigue leads to whole-body fatigue.

- High-quality glasses also provide protection against ultraviolet sunlight. Remember, you can't put sunscreen on your eyeballs.

- On rainy days, use clear or yellow lenses and wear a billed cycling cap under your helmet to shield your eyes from road spray.

- If you do get something in your eye, stop riding. It's dangerous to continue. A foreign object in one eye often causes the other eye to squint shut in a kind of muscular sympathy.

- Irrigate the affected eye immediately with water. (This is a good reason to fill at least one bottle with water rather than sports drink.) Don't delay! Blinking your eye with something in it can scratch the cornea.

IF THESE REMEDIES DON'T WORK

- If the feeling persists that your eye is scratched or something is still in it, see a physician.

Concussion

DESCRIPTION

A concussion results from a blow to the head. The brain is banged against the skull, causing swelling.

Mild concussions sometimes produce a short loss of consciousness. They also can cause amnesia or emotional problems. Severe concussions result in prolonged unconsciousness and many more-dangerous symptoms. Immediate medical care is essential.

SYMPTOMS

- If you don't lose consciousness, you may be stunned momentarily but eventually feel like you can continue riding.

- You may have seen a flash of light when your head made contact with the ground.

- A cracked helmet is a sign that you might have a serious head injury.

CAUSE

- You struck your head. Sometimes your head contacts the ground first, as in a fall over the handlebar. In sliding falls on your side, your head may whiplash into the pavement.

TREATMENT

- Stop riding immediately, even if you feel okay after the crash. If you're alone and must ride or walk home, go very slowly. You may suddenly get dizzy or find your eyes unable to focus.

- Even a brief loss of consciousness means you should see a physician.

- If you didn't lose consciousness, see how you feel the next day. If you experience headache, dizziness or nausea, go to your doctor or an emergency room.

- Don't take aspirin. If there's bleeding inside your skull, aspirin will retard clotting and can cause complications.

- If you live alone, tell a friend that you hit your head so he (or she) can check on you.

- Get medical clearance before riding again.

- If your friend falls hard and is knocked out, stabilize his head and neck, but do it with as little movement as possible. There could be a spinal cord injury. Monitor his pulse and breathing until help arrives.

TIP **Every cyclist should receive First Responder training as promoted by the American Red Cross. This will enable you to help yourself and others in emergencies. Update the course every two years.**

Serious crashes are relatively rare in cycling, but they do happen. There's no feeling so wrenching as the one you'll get while standing helpless, not knowing what to do, while another rider lies motionless on the ground.

Chapter 11
Overtraining and Recovery

I've experienced overtraining as a cyclist. I've studied it as a student. And I treat athletes for it at the Boulder Center for Sports Medicine.

But I'm still not sure what overtraining is. Is it physical, psychological or merely hype? In my experience, it's a combination of all three.

Basically, *overtraining* (sometimes called *overreaching*) is a lessening of performance despite hard training. Causes include:

- Doing too much training (including racing) without adequate rest and recovery.

- Doing intense training without a sufficient mileage base.

- Poor nutrition, especially failure to consume enough carbohydrate to replenish *glycogen* (muscle fuel) in time for the next workout.

One thing is certain—different cyclists react to the same training program in widely different ways.

A genetically gifted athlete often can tolerate huge training loads and improve steadily. But when a more modestly talented rider tries to duplicate that program, he'll probably become exhausted rather than faster.

Also, a comfortable training load one year may be too much for an athlete the next year, due to outside demands such as job and family.

Symptoms of Overtraining

The effects of overtraining can accumulate like a snowball rolling down a hill.

Typically, overtraining starts when a cyclist is feeling great, training well and improving each week. These successes fuel his desire to train harder. He might decide to restrict calorie intake to lose weight and climb better.

Then, gradually and without significant warning signs, something goes wrong. His desire for riding lessens. He has a strong urge to quit during races. His performances get worse instead of better.

Unless he knows the subtle symptoms of overtraining and takes immediate action, he'll continue to train hard—and the pattern of chronic exhaustion and poor performance will deepen.

You can see why it's vital to recognize overtraining. Here are seven key signs:

- **Steadily worsening performance**. When your performance deteriorates *despite* hard training, it's probably getting worse *because* of hard training.

- **Depression**. Psychologists have found many correlations between overtraining and symptoms of depression. In fact, William Morgan, M.D., who pioneered this research in the 1970s, once said, "I've never seen an overtrained athlete who wasn't clinically depressed." However, the exact cause-and-effect relationship is still argued in professional circles. Does overtraining cause depression, or does depression limit our capability for heavy training and high performance? The jury is still out.

- **Persistent soreness in muscles and joints**. Cycling is a non-weight-bearing activity and doesn't involve the pounding of sports involving running. For this reason, your muscles shouldn't get excessively sore even after hard rides, and they certainly shouldn't stay sore for days at a time.

- **Loss of appetite combined with a five-percent loss of body weight over several days.** Abrupt weight loss is usually a symptom of chronic dehydration. But it may also mean that your body lacks sufficient glycogen to fuel your training—and it has begun to devour muscle tissue for fuel.

- **Digestive problems including diarrhea or constipation.** Chronic fatigue can cause the digestive system to function improperly.

- **Rise in resting heart rate**. An increase of 7-10 beats above your normal morning resting heart rate is a classic symptom of overtraining.

- **Rise in white blood cell count** with accompanying susceptibility to infection and illness. This can be an excellent measure of your overtraining status if you know your white cell count under normal circumstances.

TIP **Get a complete blood count four times a year so you can establish your baseline levels.**

Causes of Overtraining

What makes athletes drive themselves to the point of overtraining? Two popular theories are goal orientation and exercise addiction.

- **Competitive, goal-oriented people are more likely to suffer from overtraining**. Their high motivation level allows them to ignore pain and discomfort. They are often high-control individuals, grasping for mastery in a world that seems to fly by out of their direct influence. A daily ride is something they can control, this control is gratifying, and so they overdo it.

- **People can develop an addiction to physical activity, especially endurance exercise.** This has been studied for decades. You've probably heard the term "runner's high." Humans produce opiates, the most common being endorphins, which are morphine-like substances secreted by the brain and pituitary gland during exercise. In theory, an addiction to these endorphins drives people to train when tired or injured.

Prevention of Overtraining

Avoiding overtraining requires several simple techniques. Trouble is, they seem to be very hard for many serious cyclists to implement:

- **Train moderately and systematically**. The body doesn't like sudden increases in mileage. Plan gradual increases and stick to your plan. There's no need to pile on massive miles, either, unless you're riding ultramarathon events. Total yearly mileage doesn't correlate well with the number of championship medals on your mantle.

- **Keep a training diary.** If you fall victim to overtraining but haven't kept a training log, you won't have a record of what you did wrong.

Write down details of your daily workout, your morning body weight, morning heart rate and a subjective rating of how you feel each day. Also include other factors such as changes to your position or equipment.

- **Beware of overtraining's symptoms**. Check the list above and monitor your body (and your mind) for early indicators of trouble. When they surface, back off your training immediately!

- **Eat and drink enough**. Many times, the cause of overtraining boils down to undereating. If you don't consume enough carbohydrate (and total calories) to fuel your training load, your muscles will fail to replenish their glycogen stores overnight. You'll build a progressively larger fuel deficit. Soon you'll be running on empty. Also, most endurance athletes are chronically dehydrated. Drink even when you aren't thirsty. You should need to urinate every couple of hours, and your urine should be nearly clear.

- **Schedule rest into your yearly training plan**. Every cyclist, no matter how enthusiastic about his sport, needs some down time. Plan periods of a week or a month where you enjoy activities other than cycling. It's fine to ride a little during this active rest, but do it only for grins and keep the intensity low.

- **Don't forget to have fun on the bike!** A bicycle is one of the best playthings humans have ever invented. So play! If every ride is a grim-faced quest to achieve goals, you'll soon know what overtraining is all about. And then you'll probably quit.

Recovery Techniques

Overtraining can be sidestepped with sound recovery techniques, too. Pro riders can go hard day after day in three-week stage races because they make a science out of recuperation.

Proper diet and hydration are important, of course. Your muscles must be well fueled for the next day's effort. But there are three other effective—and underused—recovery techniques that can make a big difference in how you feel (and ride) each day.

Leg Elevation

The simplest and most effective recovery technique takes little time and no effort.

Simply elevate your legs after a ride (photo). The lymph system, which collects liquid debris in your blood, cleanses itself more readily with an assist from gravity. Just think of the lymph system as a sewer for your body. You fill it up with waste products during a hard ride, then help it drain by raising your legs.

Yes, this is training! It's the way to finish each ride.

Lie on your back on the floor or a bed, with your butt about three feet from a wall, couch, table, or something else that's high. Raise your legs so they're at about a 45-degree angle with your heels against the object. Bend you knees slightly. Place a pillow under your head so you're comfortable. Relax. Ten minutes will work wonders.

Elevate your legs any time it's possible within the bounds of decorum and decency. For instance, prop them on a chair at dinner. Watch TV in a reclining chair rather than sitting on the couch with your feet on the floor. Soon, your family will get used to your unorthodox postures.

TIP **To make use of every chance to help your legs recover from rides, follow the pro racers' rule: Never stand when you can sit, never sit when you can lie down.**

Stretching

Although some riders make a ritual of the pre-ride stretch, it isn't especially important. Stretching is more effective when the muscles are loose—the situation after a ride, not before. So warm up on the bike with easy spinning, do the ride and then stretch afterwards when your muscles are warm and relaxed.

Stretch slowly and gradually. The mechanism of the stretch reflex is based on a little nerve ending in the tendons called the *Golgi Body*. It looks like a coiled snake. When the Golgi Body is deformed rapidly, it sends a signal to the brain for the muscle to shorten and protect itself. That's why rapid, forceful "ballistic" stretching doesn't work.

If you deform the Golgi Body rapidly, it will automatically tighten the muscle. Instead of effective stretching that produces elongation, you'll get the opposite result when your muscles contract. On the other hand, when the muscle is warm and fatigued, the Golgi Body is much more relaxed. If you go slowly, you'll get a better stretch.

For a sports-specific stretching program, consult a book on the subject. The classic in this field is Bob Anderson's book, *Stretching*, (www.stretching.com).

If you have difficulty with tendinitis or want more flexibility so you can lower your stem for better aerodynamics, you may want a more individualized stretching program. Consult a physical therapist or athletic trainer.

Self-Massage

Massage therapy is an effective recovery tool. It works because it's a manual evacuation of the lymph system and mechanical release of muscle spasms. Any pro rider can tell you that massage is an important arrow in his quiver of recovery techniques.

Pro teams employ enough massage therapists so every rider gets a nightly session on the table. For recreational rides or tours, the massage tent is the busiest place at the finish of each day's ride. But a daily or weekly massage is expensive if you aren't a pro. Fortunately, self-massage is a good option.

Although shaving is a personal choice, hairless legs are easier to massage. Hair irritates your hands and the rubbing motion can inflame hair follicles, leading to infection. Also, massage lotion coats the hair and is hard to clean off.

Use lotion so your hands glide more smoothly on the skin. Massage oil is best but moisturizing creams work well, too.

Sit on the floor in a relaxed position with your knees bent and your back supported. Start the massage with your toes and feet. Pay particular attention to the arch.

Work on the big muscle of the calf with long, sweeping strokes from the ankle toward the knee. If you find any sore areas, take more time to knead them gently.

Spend most of your massage time on the prime movers of cycling—your quads. Again, work from the knee toward your heart with long, kneading strokes. Don't forget the hamstrings, especially in the middle of the thigh and near the top where they connect to the glutes.

Chapter 12
Weight Loss

Pro cyclists are strikingly lean. Body fat percentages for elite male riders average from 3 to 10 percent while elite women average about 5 percentage points higher.

Women tend to carry extra fat for genetic reasons related to energy reserves for childbearing. Even so, hard-training women endurance athletes are now approaching male body fat percentages.

Pro riders often make a fetish out of weight loss. Low body weight improves climbing, and the improvement is greater than can be gained from many performance-enhancing drugs.

A study at Marshall University showed that one pound of bodyweight is equivalent to a one-percent difference in performance on a hilly course. In other words, if you lose a pound, your performance improves by one percent. If you gain a pound, you'll be one percent slower.

No wonder pro riders get fanatical about their weight! Lance Armstrong, in his book, *It's Not About the Bike*, reveals that he weighs his food portions. He figures that if he can monitor the exact number of calories he is ingesting and calculate the caloric expenditure of his rides, he can create a small but significant daily caloric deficit. Thus, he can lose excess weight slowly so his performance won't suffer.

CAUTION! **Several dangers can accompany attempts to reach an extremely low level of body fat:**

- **Lack of enough energy to train**. It's crucial to eat enough carbohydrate so your body can make sufficient glycogen to fuel its muscles. If you don't eat enough, first you'll burn excess fat. Then your body will begin to devour its own protein in the form of your muscles. And those muscles, in case you haven't noticed, are what propel you down the road. On the other hand, you won't lose weight unless you're incurring a calorie deficit.

The trick is to keep the deficit within reason. If you burn 500 more calories per day than you consume, you'll lose a pound every seven days. That's sensible.

- **Poor morale**. Starvation is no fun. If you're suffering from hunger or are so weak from lack of food that your rides degenerate into plodding death marches, you'll lose your enthusiasm for weight loss (and for cycling) in a hurry. The result is often binge eating when your willpower evaporates. Cycling can be a hard sport. Don't make it even tougher by trying to cut too much weight too quickly.

- **Psychological problems such as anorexia and bulimia**. In extreme cases, some cyclists may be so obsessed with weight loss that they develop eating disorders. These afflictions usually target women, and studies estimate that about one third of college female athletes have some sort of problem eating pattern.

  Psychologically predisposed men can suffer, too. About 30 percent of male athletes in body-weight-restrictive sports such as crew and wrestling are estimated to be afflicted. If you develop symptoms—episodes of binge eating, self-induced vomiting after meals, strict fasting, lack of control over your eating behavior—seek medical help immediately.

Is it possible to lose excess pounds responsibly and settle at your ideal cycling weight? Sure. Here's how:

- **Find your body fat percentage**. It's possible to be overweight but not over-fat. Muscular athletes, especially those with highly developed upper bodies, aren't too fat to be good climbers even though they may be quite heavy for their height. It's the extra muscle that slows them.

  Because it's unwise to attempt to lose muscle tissue, it's important to know how much fat weight you can safely shed. The best way is to get a body fat analysis at a university's human performance lab or at a sports medicine clinic.

- **Determine your ideal cycling weight**. When you have your body fat measured, you'll get a written analysis telling you exactly how many pounds of fat you're carrying. Often, these programs will suggest an "ideal" weight for you. These figures are only suggestions. You'll have to find your own best cycling weight by carefully monitoring how you feel and how well you perform at different weights. Less is definitely not better if you get so lean that you lose the muscle mass that's crucial to cycling performance.

- **Watch your food intake**. If you're having trouble losing unwanted fat or maintaining your ideal cycling weight once you've reached it, you are probably eating too many fat calories. It's probably the ice cream.

- **Raise your metabolism through training**. The more you ride, the more you have to eat in order to maintain your energy and supply working muscles with glycogen. Racers in three-week tours and recreational cyclists on cross-state rides or in heavy training are often astonished at the number of calories they need just to keep going. So boosting your mileage is a great way to elevate your metabolism. Cycling burns an average of about 40 calories per mile, meaning a century incinerates around 4,000 calories.

- **Incorporate mild exercise into your normal day** if you can't ride more miles due to time constraints. Use the stairs instead of the elevator. Take a brisk walk at lunch. Ride your bike a mile to the convenience store rather than taking the car. Skip the morning snack break and walk 10 flights of stairs instead. Every little bit helps.

- **Commute to work**. Riding your bike to work is a great way to elevate your metabolism all day. The morning commute fires up your fat-burning mechanisms. The ride home in the afternoon assures that you'll be feeding more excess fat to your internal furnaces all evening and through the night.

- **Ride the trainer in the morning**. Two or three times a week, hit the trainer or rollers for 30 minutes first thing in the morning, just before breakfast. There's no need to go hard. A moderate spin is fine. This trick is an easy way to get your metabolic fires stoked so you burn additional fat all day. After the spin, eat a sensible low-fat breakfast.

TIP **Begin weight control measures in the winter so you arrive at spring closer to your ideal cycling weight. Then as you increase your training, fine-tune your weight to find your best performance level.**

Chapter 13
Physiological Testing

Every sport has performance parameters that distinguish top athletes from those who are less gifted.

Basketball players pride themselves on their vertical jumps. NFL cornerbacks vie to run the fastest 40-yard dash. Linemen compete in the bench press.

After years of testing athletes, coaches and physiologists now know the performance levels that identify athletes most likely to succeed.

Cycling has performance tests, too. Of course, you can enjoy riding without knowing your numbers. But it's important to find out how you stack up if you're interested in top performance so you (or your coach) can devise a training program to help you improve.

If you use a heart rate monitor, you're wasting time if you don't undergo performance testing. By knowing your numbers for your lactate threshold, you can designate heart rate ranges for different intensity levels. For this reason, many serious cyclists choose to get tested at a sports medicine clinic or university human performance lab.

Performance Testing

Here are several basic performance tests for cyclists:

VO$_2$ max

Maximum oxygen uptake, or VO$_2$ max, is a measure of how efficiently your working muscles can use oxygen.

It's usually expressed in milliliters of oxygen per kilogram of body weight. Top male cyclists often have a VO_2 max of 70 to 80 ml/kg. Equally fit elite women tend to score about 5 ml/kg lower.

The ultimate ceiling on an individual's VO_2 max is largely inherited, but it can be improved by about 25 percent with appropriate workouts.

VO_2 max is an excellent indicator of fitness but a poor predictor of performance within a group of similar athletes. The reason—some very economical cyclists can produce more power at a given VO_2 max.

Maximum oxygen uptake can be improved with repeated efforts of 3 to 5 minutes at a heart rate of 95 percent of VO_2 max. These efforts are very demanding.

Lactate Threshold (LT)

This is the highest level of intensity you can maintain for a significant period—usually 30 to 45 minutes.

LT is expressed in different ways: as heart rate, power output in watts, velocity or percent of VO_2 max.

LT can be determined directly by taking blood samples and measuring the amount of lactic acid (*lactate*) at gradually increasing levels of effort. LT is usually defined as a concentration of 4 millimoles per liter of blood. A sudden 1-millimole jump from one level to another can indicate your threshold.

Coaches or physiologists prescribe specific exercise intensity zones based on LT.

LT can be raised with a variety of interval training efforts at or slightly above your threshold pace, as well as longer rides slightly below your LT.

Power at LT

This is measured in watts. It's the amount of power you can generate at your LT, and is one of the best predictors of endurance performance.

Power at LT can be improved with intervals at or slightly above threshold pace, combined with strength-building exercises. These include weight training and low-cadence, high-resistance intervals on short hills.

Economy

Power at LT is a good indicator of *economy*, a measure of how fast you can go at a given level of intensity.

Economy is a combination of smooth pedaling technique, strength and mechanical factors such as good aerodynamics and low rolling resistance.

You can improve your economy with pedaling drills and long intervals ridden at about 80 percent of max heart rate. Emphasize good form.

A Word about Testing Procedures

At the Boulder Center for Sports Medicine, testing is done on a stationary bike integrated with a computer. The bike has a racing-style saddle and handlebar so you can duplicate your position on your road bike.

We ask cyclists to bring their own pedals, cycling shoes and cycling shorts. We also provide instructions for preparing for the test. We want you to taper workouts the week before and not eat during the three hours preceding the test.

We attach electrodes to your chest so we can monitor your heart rate and EKG. The electrodes are held in place with a stretchy piece of gauze shaped like a sock that you pull over your upper body. You are fitted with a mask to breathe through so we can collect and analyze your oxygen use. We periodically check your blood pressure throughout the procedure.

The test starts with a low-resistance warmup. When you're ready, we increase the resistance 20 watts every three minutes. At the end of each three-minute block, we draw a small blood sample from a fingertip. Don't worry. It doesn't hurt (much). We analyze each blood sample to see how much lactate you've accumulated. When lactate levels start to rise abruptly, you've reached your lactate threshold. When that happens, we record your heart rate and wattage output.

After you reach LT, we decrease the resistance and let you pedal easily until you recover. Then, to measure VO_2 max, we increase the resistance more rapidly (usually every minute) until you can't pedal at a reasonably high rpm any longer. The computer automatically analyzes the gases you're breathing in and out to determine your VO_2 max.

After the test, a physiologist sits down with you to go over the computer-generated charts and graphs showing your performance. We make recommendations about training zones and workout plans to help you improve. This data also can be used by your coach to set up a yearlong training program with appropriate intensity levels in each season. You need to work hard enough to get better but also avoid overtraining.

Blood Testing

Many tired or under-performing cyclists want blood tests. They'd love the physician to find a single profile that is low, then remedy it with a shot or vitamin supplement.

Such happy results are rare. Most well-trained cyclists, even if their performances are in a slump, have blood test results well within the normal range.

Because a number of routine blood factors are affected by consistent training, I recommend that every cyclist get his or her blood tested two to three times a year. The purpose is to establish baseline numbers. A rider will have ranges that are normal for him, but these ranges can differ among healthy athletes, often to a large degree.

Medical professionals should interpret your numbers, so I won't include so-called "normal ranges." They can be misleading.

Here are the common elements of a blood tests and a description of what is being measured:

- **CBC** is a *complete blood count*. Iron profiles (see FERR, FE, TIBC and Sat below) monitor the blood's oxygen-carrying capacity.

- **RBC** (*red blood cells*) is measured in millions per ml of blood. Low numbers may be a sign of anemia. Training causes an increase in red cell production.

- **HG** (hemoglobin) is a protein molecule inside each red cell with an iron atom attached. The iron atom transports oxygen. Hemoglobin gives blood its red color.

- **HTC** (*hematocrit*) describes the percentage of blood that is solid cells. (The rest is fluid or plasma.) Dehydration can falsely increase this percentage because it decreases the fluid part of the blood.

  Hematocrit has been in the news recently because of a drug, EPO that increases the percent of red cells and, therefore, improves endurance performance. Because EPO use has been undetectable until recently, cycling's governing body, the UCI, decreed that anyone with a hematocrit over 50.0 was unfit to race, reasoning that the blood contained too much solid matter to be pumped efficiently and could cause cardiac problems. As a result, cyclists testing over 50.0 were suspended for two weeks until their hematocrit went down.

Unfortunately, a high hematocrit doesn't necessarily mean EPO use. Living at altitude and being dehydrated also produce readings well in excess of 50.0. At this writing, a test has finally been approved to detect EPO use directly.

- **MCV** (*mean corpuscular volume*) indicates the average size of red cells. Young, fresh cells are larger than old ones at the end of their usefulness.

- **MCH** (*mean corpuscular hemoglobin*) is the amount of hemoglobin by weight in each red cell.

- **FERR** (*ferritin*) levels indicate the level of iron being salvaged from old red cells and put back into service. Low levels of ferritin may indicate that iron is being lost from the system.

- **Fe** (*iron*) is found as part of the hemoglobin inside each red cell where oxygen is transported to the working muscles.

- **TIBC** (*total iron-binding capacity*) will be a high value when the body is mobilizing iron stores throughout the body. This may indicate a potential future deficit in stored iron reserves.

- **Sat** (saturation) indicates the blood iron concentration divided by the total iron binding capacity. Values below 20 percent indicate inadequate iron transport capacity.

The physical and mental stress of training can cause damage to the muscles, connective tissue, joints and cell membranes. Hormone levels are also affected by these mental and physical stresses. Four tests help identify problems:

- **WBC** (*white blood cells* or *leukocytes*) is measured in thousands per ml of blood. White cells protect the body against disease, so their numbers usually increase with stress, infection, viruses and inflammation. Certain vitamin deficiencies and poor diet also can affect white cell count.

- **CBC differential**. White blood cells come in several types: lymphocytes, monocytes, neutrophils, eosinophils and basophils. *CBC differential* is the ratio of these different cells. It can help your physician or physiologist determine disease.

- **Plat** (*platelets*) are cells made in bone marrow. They contain serotonin, adrenalin and histamine. These cells adhere to damaged tissue and release their contents, causing clotting.

- **Sed rate** (*sedimentation rate*) is the speed at which red blood cells settle to the bottom of their collection vessel. Damaged cells clump together. This makes them fall faster than single, healthy cells. Elevated sed rate is usually a sign of infection.

Special tests done with your blood can measure levels of certain hormones. Because individual levels of these substances differ greatly, it's important to have your individual data collected over a year or more to get an accurate picture. Common hormones that affect training include:

- **Thyroid.** Low levels lead to sluggish performance.

- **Cortisol**, a steroid produced by the adrenal glands in times of stress. There are many good effects of cortisol, but an excess indicates problems with recovery.

- **Testosterone**, an androgen steroid produced by the testes and ovaries influencing growth, development, recovery and behavior. It is six times more prevalent in males than in females. Overtraining can suppress production.

- **Cortisol-testosterone ratio**. It's thought that elevated testosterone will improve recovery, but elevated cortisol indicates chronic stress inflammation and overtraining.

- **Female hormones** (estrogen and progesterone) can be affected by training, leading to a disruption of the menstrual cycle.

Chapter 14
Health Maintenance

Every cyclist gets sick sometime. In fact, trained endurance athletes are more likely than their sedentary counterparts to become ill, usually with upper respiratory tract infections (URTI).

Studies of marathon runners show that the risk of infection rises dramatically during the 48 hours after the hard and protracted effort of running 26 miles. Their bodies' reserves are used to recover, leaving little energy to fight infection.

No one wants to lose training time (or the fun of riding) because of nagging illnesses. When is it safe to ride through an ailment? Do vitamins help you avoid getting sick? Let's close this book by looking at these key issues.

Riding Through Illness

If you catch a cold (officially an upper-respiratory tract infection), here's how to recover quickly:

- **Rest**. I know, you have plenty of responsibilities, probably a job and family, and you don't have time to rest. A day or two in bed? Forget it. But colds respond to rest because some quality loafing gives the body extra energy to fight infection. Cut back on your work hours, take a sick day, ask your spouse to take over the dishwashing chores—anything to get a little more down time when you're trying to recover.

- **Drink lots of fluids**. This is good advice at any time (most cyclists are chronically dehydrated), but it's especially important when you have a cold. Water is good, but drink fruit juices too, especially orange juice for added vitamin C.

- **Return to training gradually**. If you miss one week of training, restrict yourself to easy spinning for one week. Then gradually return to the mileage and intensity you were doing before you got sick.

CAUTION! **Nearly all over-the-counter cold remedies contain *pseudoephedrine*, a stimulant that is also a banned substance. Usually, taking a cold remedy will mean that you'll test positive for drug use. Drug testing isn't limited to elite athletes. Anyone competing at a USA Cycling-sanctioned event can be tested at any time.**

For riders not concerned about medical controls at big races, it's okay to take a cold remedy to feel better for the activities of daily life. Doing so is also appropriate when you're on a tour and need to quell cold symptoms to get through each day. Ride slow and easy so your body has the energy reserves to recover from the illness.

Because we like to ride, we usually find it hard to take time off the bike when we're ill. When is it safe to ride—and when are you better off staying off the bike to rest and pump the fluids?

Follow the above-the-neck rule. When cold symptoms are above your neck (stuffy, drippy nose), it's okay to exercise lightly. But when symptoms are below the neck (muscle aches, chest congestion, cough), don't ride.

If you feel sick and puny, it's often better to rest and recover. In the long run, you'll be farther ahead to take several days or a week off and get better before you resume training. If you try to train through a bad cold or the flu, you'll slow your recovery. Your return to form will take longer.

Vitamin Supplements

Under normal circumstances, cyclists get all the vitamins they need from their daily meals. After all, bike riders eat enormous amounts! There's no need to spend your hard-earned cash on pricey vitamins. Most vitamins are water-soluble so you just end up with expensive urine. Besides, I bet you'd like to buy a new bike with your money.

Still, for insurance purposes, I think it's wise for cyclists to take a daily vitamin supplement that contains antioxidants (vitamins A, C, E and beta-carotene). These can help recovery. I believe a supplement also should contain iron, for men as well as women.

Men have been warned to avoid iron supplements because of the danger of storing excess iron (*hemochromatosis*) but the risk has been overstated. Less than one percent of the population has this condition. If you have a family history of the disease or other concerns, consult your physician.

Women should take calcium, too. Pre-menopausal and menstruating women should take the equivalent of several Tums a day. After menopause, check with your physician about hormone replacement therapy and calcium supplements.

Acknowledgments

No body of knowledge can be compiled or subsequent book be written without the help of many people. I would like to thank those who have helped me get to where I am today

The voice and example of my parents are forever powerful. The patience of my wife Sue and son Scott, who modeled for this book, are always appreciated. The wisdom and foresight of James Holmes, M.D., was crucial to my personal and professional development.

The U.S. Cycling Federation and Chris Carmichael, who gave me the opportunity to work with the best athletes in the world, cannot be forgotten. A special thanks to my Le Peep/Celestial Seasonings Cycling Team mates, whom I have studied in depth and whose friendships I cherish. I hope that Marc, Lars, Steve, Brad, Bob and I can ride forever.

And finally to my friends, Ed Pavelka and Fred Matheny, without whom this book would never have happened. I appreciate your belief in me and this project.

To all who will listen—God bless, happy trails, and keep the rubber side down.

Andy Pruitt
July 2001

About the Authors

Andrew L. Pruitt, Ed.D.

is director of the Boulder Center for Sports Medicine in Boulder, CO (www.BCH.org/sportsmedicine). He is one of the world's foremost experts on bike fit and cycling injuries.

Pruitt headed the U.S. Cycling Federation's sports medicine program for many years, including four World Championships. He was the Chief Medical Officer for U.S. Cycling at the 1996 Olympics in Atlanta. He also helped design medical coverage for the Atlanta cycling venues on a model he developed as Medical Director of the Tour Dupont.

Pruitt is the recognized leader in computerized cycling gait analysis. This technique uses three-dimensional computer technology to determine perfect bike fit for all riders, a service available at the BCSM.

Andy began his athletic career in traditional sports—football, basketball, baseball and track. Losing the lower part of his right leg in a hunting accident at age 14 didn't stop him. He became a wrestler and high jumper, eventually winning 12 high school varsity letters. He attended Drake University and Iowa State, earning a Bachelor of Science degree in anatomy, an M.S. from the University of Colorado, and an Ed.D. from California Coast University. He became an athletic trainer at CU in 1973 and served for many years as Director of Sports Medicine.

While at CU, Pruitt began cycling and skiing. He won a bronze medal in the downhill at the U.S. Disabled Ski Championships in 1978, but found his true passion in cycling. Over a 10-year racing career, he earned a USCF Category 2 ranking competing against able-bodied riders. He won two National Championships and two World Championships as a disabled rider. He continues to compete in time trials and occasional road races. As late as 2001 he had a top-10 finish among able-bodied racers in the 50+ category of the Durango-to-Silverton Road Race.

Andy's wife Sue and teenage son Scott (the model for this book) are avid cyclists and skiers. Scott is a national-caliber junior Nordic skier as well as a road and mountain bike racer.

Fred Matheny

has written about cycling for 24 years, including six books and hundreds of articles. He is vice president of RBR Publishing Company and a prolific contributor to its Road-BikeRider.com website and free weekly newsletter. He has written three RBR books: *Basic Training for Roadies, Off-Season Training for Roadies* and *Spring Training for Roadies*.

Matheny first met Pruitt on top of the infamous "Wall" of the Morgul-Bismark road race course outside Boulder, Colorado, while they were watching a late-'70s edition of the legendary Red Zinger Classic. Since then, they have collaborated on dozens of articles and ridden countless miles together.

Matheny began cycling in the early 1970s after an athletic career that included football and track in high school and football at Baldwin-Wallace College in Ohio, where he was named all-league and his team's outstanding offensive lineman.

After he moved to Colorado in 1970, cycling helped him lose 50 pounds he had gained to play college ball. He enjoyed riding so much that it soon became his passion.

Matheny rode his first race in 1976. A category 2 racer since 1978, his top placings include a cat 3 win in the Mount Evans Hill Climb; a world record of 5 days, 11 hours in the 1996 Team Race Across America; first place in the Colorado Masters Time Trial Championships; and third place at the 2000 Masters National Time Trial Championships.

Matheny and his wife of 33 years, Debbie, live in Montrose, Colorado. Their son Ross is following family tradition by embarking on a career in teaching.

Other Readings

Edmund Burke, Ph.D., *High-Tech Cycling*

Edmund Burke, Ph.D., *Science of Cycling*

Clinics in Sports Medicine, "Bicycling Injuries," Jan. '94

Davis Phinney/Connie Carpenter, *Training for Cycling*